SEEING LIKE A CHILD

Thinking from Elsewhere

Series editors:

Clara Han, Johns Hopkins University, and
Bhrigupati Singh, Ashoka University

International Advisory Board

Roma Chatterji, University of Delhi
Veena Das, Johns Hopkins University
Robert Desjarlais, Sarah Lawrence College
Harri Englund, Cambridge University
Didier Fassin, Institute for Advanced Study, Princeton
Angela Garcia, Stanford University
Junko Kitanaka, Keio University
Eduardo Kohn, McGill University
Heonik Kwon, Cambridge University
Michael Lambek, University of Toronto
Deepak Mehta, Ashoka University, Sonepat
Amira Mittermaier, University of Toronto
Sameena Mulla, Marquette University
Marjorie Murray, Pontificia Universidad Católica de Chile
Young-Gyung Paik, Jeju National University
Sarah Pinto, Tufts University
Michael Puett, Harvard University
Fiona Ross, University of Cape Town
Lisa Stevenson, McGill University

Seeing Like a Child

INHERITING THE KOREAN WAR

Clara Han

FORDHAM UNIVERSITY PRESS   NEW YORK 2021

Fordham University Press has no responsibility for the
persistence or accuracy of URLs for external or third-
party internet websites referred to in this publication and
does not guarantee that any content on such websites is,
or will remain, accurate or appropriate.

Fordham University Press also publishes its books in a
variety of electronic formats. Some content that appears
in print may not be available in electronic books.

Visit us online at www.fordhampress.com.

Library of Congress Cataloging-in-Publication Data
available online at https://catalog.loc.gov.

Printed in the United States of America

23 22 21   5 4 3 2 1

First edition

For Mom 차정화 *and Dad* 한숙종
For Ella

Contents

Foreword

Richard Rechtman

Has anybody ~~has~~ ever lived The Big Story the way it is written in books and printed for collective memory? Of course not. It does not exist. History, with a capital "H," is just an artifact to build a collective story that never actually happened that way for the individual. Of course, each individual participates and contributes to The Big Story. Each experience possesses elements of The Big Story. But the way each one lives it remains a purely subjective experience that, sometimes, has very little in common with what we call The Big Story. It is possible to understand and write The Big Story precisely because science has been able to extract out the singular and subjective experience of major events.

Thanks to research in history, sociology, anthropology, political science, and so on for bringing us an understanding of our collective past, and sometimes our present. There is no better way to describe how we proceed to grasp this sense of collective destiny than Claude Lévi-Strauss's concluding remarks of *The Naked Man*, the fourth volume of *The Mythologiques*. What he says about myth and its complex

relationship with subjectivity can be extrapolated to collective
memory and to The Big Story. Both are individual, complex
expressions, but they become collective through the process
of erasing all individual subjectivity. If myth exists and spreads
over time, Lévi-Strauss writes, it is not so much because it
was invented by Man or someone, as great as he or she could
be. On the contrary, it is the narrative form that owes nothing to an enlightened or poetic consciousness—that is, to the
expression of a subjectivity (Rechtman 1996). Myth is precisely different from other oral or literary narrative forms. It
derives its permanence from internal logic alone, not emotional or semantic involvement, which is otherwise attached
to these forms. Lévi-Strauss explains this masterfully by emphasizing that every myth has its origin in an individual creation, but "to pass to the state of myth," he adds, "it is precisely
necessary that a creation does not remain individual and
loses, during this promotion, the essential factors due to the
probability that would initially impede it and that one could
attribute to the temperament, talent, imagination and personal experiences of its author" (Lévi-Strauss 1971, 559). We
could replace myth by The Big Story and then get a clear
definition of the process through which a sense of collective
memory is created. Collective memory is much less the product of individual consciousness than the narrative framework
that allows each individual to format his or her unique experience in accordance with that of his or her home group. And
this is precisely what we do as researchers: we try to discover
how people interact with the collective narrative of The Big
Story or collective memory and then express their own destiny through this pattern. But in ordinary life, this is not the
way it really works.

   In real life, people do not make a clear hierarchy between
what affects them in ordinary life for inner reasons and what

affects them as a consequence of what we call The Big Story until long after the fact.

Other than in literature, this issue has been neglected in academic studies, especially in social sciences, for many different reasons. Obviously, from an empirical point of view, it is quite difficult to get sufficient data to document the oscillation in the ordinary between personal or idiosyncratic feelings, preoccupations, fears, and anxiety and those that could be connected to major events in collective life. The descent into the ordinary, to borrow Veena Das's concept, is probably the most powerful tool to get in touch with this discrete reality of everyday life (Das 2007; Das 2015a). But even with the utmost sensitivity to others, to their forms of life, and whatever the length of time one could spend with others, one could never get as close as to one's own inner reality. And this is exactly the purpose of this amazing book *Seeing Like a Child*. It is nothing less than Clara Han's challenge to reach this otherwise elusive ordinary reality.

Seeing Like a Child is a moving account of what should be named as an unexpected voice from a confirmed researcher. It is much more a kind of automemory, than an autobiography. It shows how life between two very different worlds is crossed by an inner exile that truly exists but without the vocabulary or the facts to express it. Just as if something is missing, but without the memory of what it was. A pure blank, I should say. Clara's writing is like a journey into the deepest lack that leaves a blank in a child's memory. We travel with her, without knowing where she will go or what she will find. That is the challenge of this journey. From the United States to Korea, by asking questions, sharing intimate moments, and visiting unknown relatives, she is not only searching for historical facts that are still missing in her memory, she is searching for feelings, impressions, smells, and attitudes that could organically fit what she perceived when she was young, but without having the knowledge to name them at that time.

§

Here, the usual questions—where do I come from, who am I, why am I here and not elsewhere, where does my family come from—take a very singular and specific resonance because they are objectively unsolved questions. They are material facts and not just imaginary fantasy. But even if the facts are missing, the fantasy keeps on searching for reality. That is the main difference with what Freud calls "Family Romance." It does not mean that there is no Family Romance among second or third generations of refugees. There is, of course. But this very specific context of exile gives an accent of reality to this neurotic search. Children born from an anonymous sperm donor also have a fantasy of a Family Romance, but when it occurs, it has a particular coloration that results more or less directly from this knowledge of an origin by assisted reproductive technology, which has something to do with the medical reality of their procreation. Discovering this reality (i.e., the biological father is an anonymous sperm donor) does not change the need of a fantasy of a Family Romance. In a Family Romance, children usually invent other parents for themselves, most of the time richer and smarter than their own. Medical insemination does not suppress the fantasy; rather, it gives a possible reality. The difference remains in the fact that while it remains a fantasy, it looks even more like a possible reality. The usual enigma of the origin of oneself is replaced by a pseudocertitude. For example: Who do I come from? Is my father really my father? Is my mother my real mother or am I born from someone else who has been hidden from me? These become obsolete questions since the child knows that these parents are not his or her biological parents. The reality of medically

assisted procreation does not stifle the fantasy of the Family
Romance. The child born from medically assisted procreation knows that these parents are not his biological parents,
but that does not prevent him from dreaming that he has had
others even more famous than his own. That is the only difference with the ordinary neurotic: this knowledge on their
origin probably makes the fantasy last, but it does not pro-
duce it.

§

In the case of exile, one could find something quite similar.
It is not the origin of life but the origin of the family that is
questioned. Who were they before, why did they escape,
what have they done, were they heroes or victims, have
they done something wrong, or is it their family that has
done something wrong? So many questions that the ordinary neurotic does not generally ask, at least not in this
way. This is because the second-generation child may want
to find the truth and then explore the past to fill the lacking
information.

   In this respect, Clara Han is not searching for facts or to
obtain a full family history. She is trying to give an account
of what her eyes at the time could have seen and how those
impressions can, nowadays, be connected to an emotional
reality rather than a historical reality.

§

This is probably the point where the singular history crosses
The Big Story. In this case, when one does not know the reason why one is here and not elsewhere, it is not just a neurotic question (like we all share), it is often a political reality
that has projected this family to where they are. A political
history that belongs to previous generations but affects sub-
sequent generations, even long after the fact. This could be
the definition of exile for the second and third generations:
they are overwhelmed by The Big Story that leaves traces and

scars, but not the memory of the facts, only feelings, emotions, sensations, or all kinds of unqualified anxiety.

§

This is exactly the path Clara asks us to follow with her. Step by step, she rediscovers her family, her language, the habits of her parents' country of origin. Little by little, we perceive how The Big Story had transformed their own world and how it has distilled habits in her parents, habits that are otherwise incomprehensible.

§

In her search through her missing past world, she is looking for all kind of traces, even though she knows that none could restore the whole narrative of the past. So instead of presenting a full account rebuilt by mixing academic knowledge, fragments of memories, *après-coup* reconstruction, she gives us a fragment of her own reality, of her own subjectivity, just as it comes to her during this journey through her past.

Here, subjectivity is less the psychological assumption of a "self-consciousness" than the strange feeling of being absolutely sure that she is the one who is affected by what is happening, without knowing what this "she," or should I say "I," really means.

This artifact is probably the best way, even the only one, to get in touch with the ordinary, and to write it just as it comes, like the anthropologist exploring an undiscovered country with the main difference that, in this case, the field is her own family. Being part of the ethnographic scene but not the focus point, almost as if she were only wide-open eyes, seeing what is there and what is hidden.

Writing a book like this opens at least three major theoretical perspectives.

First of all, seeing the world like a child means trying to write from this singular experience. It supposes writing without the deepness of history, without knowing what will be

important later and what will be considered as the premise
of the future. It means writing as the present emerges before
any awareness. This has something to do with children's cognitive mind, of course, but this also happens in many other
contexts of life, even if children give the usual illustration.
In other words, writing without anticipation of the future
deepness of history could be the paradigmatic definition of
writing the ordinary. Writing without knowing the end of the
story, without knowing which place each event will take in
the full story. Writing just like things were perceived at the
very moment they emerged. But what does it mean, for example, to live in a society where commemoration and memories are key points? What does it mean for people who lose
memory, like Clara's father, or like a child who does not live
through memory? The answer lays probably in the second
consequence: writing in the first person.

Seeing Like a Child is less a personal journey through intimate thoughts written in the first person than an essay on
what it means to say "I" instead of "we" or "us" and what
doing so changes for anthropology. As I said before, the use
of the first person is not the premise of a self-consciousness.
It is just the statement of an irreducible subjectivity that stems
from the simple fact of saying "I." The one who says "I" simply claims that the subjectivity that appears only belongs to
the one saying "I," but without any qualification of who or
what is this first person. A purely grammatical subjectivity
completely connected to the linguistic reality that nobody
can say "I" instead of me. If someone wishes to use this first
person (mine) to pretend to talk as if she were me, it would
be her own subjectivity. So, for me, each time someone says
"I" it only means "he" or "she." This is exactly what Émile
Benveniste demonstrates in his famous paper on subjectivity in language (Benveniste 1966). This perspective has further consequences, in particular on the qualification of

subjectivity and its possible disappearance, especially with death. In his book *Donner la mort* (Giving death), Jacques Derrida underlines the fact that "nobody can die instead of me," which defines the paradigmatic radicality of subjectivity.[1] It means that in facing death nobody can replace me (Derrida 1999). The first person is coextensive with a grammatical subjectivity that precedes any self-consciousness. In other words, before being able to recognize that Ego is me, one has to say "I." The syntagma "I am me" corresponds to the declarative statement of a subjectivity that is nothing else than the possibility that the one who says "I" is me.

In ordinary life, the first person and Ego are intimately connected and, in fact, substitutable. Furthermore, in English the use of "I" and "me" defines indifferently the subject of the enunciation and the object of the statement.

In this regard, death introduces a radical separation between these two forms. The grammatical expression of subjectivity, the pronoun "I," always disappears before self-consciousness. As human beings, we lose the capacity of saying "I" before having the knowledge of this loss. Death is then a pure and radical experience of subjectivity, in the fact that no one else can have this experience for me. At the very moment of the end of my life, the first person always disappears before me. I will never be able to say "I am dead." Death is then the real disappearance of the subjectivity, while Ego will never be able to know that. There is no self-consciousness of death, because the subject of the enunciation ("I") always disappears before the object of the statement ("me"). Freud expresses this paradox through this classic formula: "There is no possible representation of one own's death" (Freud 1989 [1915]). In other words, Ego will never have any knowledge of the reality of its disappearance and will not have any representation of this paradoxical reality.

But what happens when self-consciousness is not already there or disappears before the subject of enunciation? According to the previous definition, as far as "I," the first person as a subject, is present, it is not death, rather a form of life different from the usual one. In other words, what is a life with no awareness of the past and, moreover, no need to refer to any kind of personal or collective past, although the subject of the enunciation is still present: an "I" with no "me."

This issue leads to the third consequence raised by Clara Han's book. It is about memory and our modern sense of identity in relation to this oscillation between the subject of the enunciation ("I") and the object, the self-consciousness as a social construction. If the paradox between the first person as subject of enunciation and object of the statement defines all human being, it has some exceptions. In childhood, for instance, the self-consciousness is less a process of knowledge than a kind of performative declaration of the first person. "Seeing like a child" is therefore a way to express the existence of a first person, Clara Han's "I," at a time where memory, history, and even past were not required to define Ego. This is the strong affirmation of a grammatical subjectivity that can be read throughout the book. It is a way to question the need of a past history and, furthermore, of a memory to qualify the modern subject, which is in fact only a social construction. For children, saying "I" is clearly sufficient to have the sense of being. There is no need at this age for any other construction of an inner psychological reality, and especially no need for them to have the knowledge of a personal or family past history.

Aging and dementia share quite the same relationship with memory and past history. This is the reason why Clara's book is so powerful in its attempt to demonstrate, and perform at the same time, how we, in our modern world, associate self-consciousness, identity, memory, and personal and collective past history.

In dementia, at the opposite of biological death, where "I" (the subject of the enunciation) disappears before "me" (the self-consciousness), here "me" disappears while "I" is still there. It could be the paradigmatic definition of social death in our modern language. A pure Subject of enunciation with no self-consciousness because there is no more memory.

§

Through the metaphor of *seeing like a child*, Clara Han reveals like no one before her the strength of this social construction between identity, memory, and self-consciousness in ordinary life.

SEEING LIKE A CHILD

Introduction

The writer Han Kang opens her memoir with a list of white things (Han 2018). White swaddling bands that wrapped a baby, her older sister, who died just two hours after being born. A newborn gown, sewn frantically by her mother as she was going into premature labor. It is worn as the baby flits open her eyes and as she closes them with her last breaths. Snow falls in a blizzard in Seoul overwhelming an umbrella. It falls in a strange city covering over footprints just made. Snow seeps into ash covering that city obliterated by war, the city where Han Kang writes these words. She continues, "With each item, I wrote down, a ripple of agitation ran through me. I felt that yes, I needed to write this book, and that the process of writing it would be transformative, would itself transform, into something like a white ointment applied to a swelling, like a gauze laid over a wound. Something I needed" (Han 2016, 6).

The starkness in white, the promise in white, white's life and lethality, shudder forth in small fragile things. They leave impressions. A white pebble found on a beach a long time ago: "If silence could be condensed into the smallest, most solid object, this is how it would feel" (Han 2016, 101). A sugar cube, seen for the first time when she accompanied her aunt to a coffee shop, "still evokes the sense of witnessing something precious" (93). White grains of rice "lie quiet in her bag as she carries them home" (133). A handkerchief falls while a woman is hanging her washing from a balcony rail, "like a bird with its wings half furled. Like a soul tentatively sounding out a place it might alight" (83). These impressions are not the writer's alone. They are shared with her sister, who comes alive through the labor of putting words to white paper, a gift to her, an acknowledgment of drawing her sister's "final breath" (161).

Han Kang describes her sister's birth, her glimpse of life, and her death multiple times. She begins one such description with "She grew up inside this story" (Han 2016, 125). What follows is a description of her sister's birth in the third person. "She was born prematurely, at seven months . . ." (125). Yet, it is unclear who the "she" is in "She grew up inside this story." Is "she" Han Kang, whose existence is shadowed by her sister's death, or her sister, who grew up—as Han Kang grew up—from within this story of her birth and death? But it is also unclear to what "this story" refers. Is it the story of the baby's birth and death, the story of carrying a mother's ashes to the temple, the story of a city devastated by war, or a story of washing pills down to soften excruciating pain? Is it all of these stories or none of them? Han Kang leaves us with these open questions, allowing us to string together, as children do, a cat's cradle of impressions.

§

I am drawn to the intense simplicity of Han Kang's descriptions, a simplicity in which household items such as grains of rice or a handkerchief, or a momentary freezing of water on the windowsill, are both illuminated and shadowed by wonder and grief that is both her world's and the world's. Such simplicity does not involve the smoothing down of texture to reveal an underlying truth. Rather, the texture is that simplicity—the difficulty of perception resides in the fact that it is right before us. Such simplicity is a route to self-knowledge, the writing itself transforming the writer. Can this self-knowledge also be anthropological knowledge?

In this book, I explore the ways in which the catastrophic event of the Korean War is dispersed into a domestic life marked by small corrosions and devastating loss. I do this by writing from the inside of my childhood memories, and by responding to these memories as an adult, such that the adult reflections come as a response to—but not overwriting of— the childhood memory. I write as the daughter of parents who were displaced by war, who fled from the North to the South of Korea, and whose displacement in Korea and sub- sequent migration to the United States implicated the fray- ing and suppression of kinship relations and the Korean language. I write as a mother of a daughter living with her grandfather—my father—who is increasingly debilitated by dementia, such that she is learning illness and dying as part and parcel of learning what a grandfather is, what care is, what the world is. But, I also write as an anthropologist whose fieldwork has taken me to the devastated worlds of my parents—to Korea and to the Korean language—allowing me to find and found kinship relationships that had been suppressed or broken in war and illness.

Through the overlapping of autobiography and ethnogra- phy, I attempt to see like a child (again) who is puzzling together words and tidbits of perceptions and, in doing so, learning kinship, violence, affliction, and death. Seeing like a child can provide a different route by which anthro- pology comes to understand and receive the inheritance of catastrophe within kinship and family. For the child "learns language and world together" and does not have recourse to stable categories of thought that adults may rely on to narrativize and create boundaries around "the event." Instead, [the child is simply learning what the world is, but that world and that everyday life already bear the traces of war and devastation.] Thus, the event, for the child, cannot be a priori treated as marked out from the fabric of everyday life. On the contrary, it is completely interspersed within it. Thus, [in counterpoint to the project of testimony that seeks to transmit a narrative of the event to future generations, *Seeing Like a Child* sees the inheritance of familial memories of violence as embedded in the child's inhabitation of everyday life.] This body of writing is my response to this everyday life, its loss, and its fragile reinhabitation.

Witnessing and Memory

My childhood memories found their way into writing in conversation with my friend and colleague Andrew Brandel, whose grandparents were survivors of the Nazi genocide. We began a project of writing together, sharing our childhood memories in relation to war and genocide that have marked our families. Through the back and forth of our writings, we began to see how scenes of inheritance of these memories of violence—what we called a "genre of the child witness"— distinguished themselves from the standing literature on family memory and the intergenerational transmission of trauma. That is, by putting our childhood memories next to each other, we began to see a different picture of inheritance emerge, one in which "children are piecing together a world from the bits of social life that they find around them" such that the fragments of experience of war and genocide are not marked out from everyday life but rather dispersed within that life (Han and Brandel 2019). At the same time, we took the child not as a developmental stage that culminates in adulthood, in which mastery over a narrative is gained. Instead, the child could be understood as a "stage" that could be reactivated at any point in one's lifetime, allowing us to engage in a relearning of a world and, thus, to claim a voice in that world (see Cavell 2008).

This method of seeing like a child—to follow the childhood memory as a route into the child's world-in-the-making—marks the genre out from the standing literature on the transmission of memory within the site of the family. Consider Jan and Aleida Assmann's notions of "communicative memory" and "cultural memory" in which the individual, family, and nation appear as nested units. "Communicative memory" is understood as "everyday communications" at the level of the household that shares a "common image of their past." Such memory, further, has a "limited temporal horizon" that matches the assumed biological lifespan of one generation (eighty to one hundred years) (A. Assmann 2009; J. Assmann 1995; J. Assmann 2007; see also Erll 2011). While communicative memory is spatially bound into the household, "cultural memory" is that memory that is articulated at the level of the public sphere. It arises out of a compulsion or "need for identity." Here, a rather teleological picture is assumed in which older generations are compelled to create institutional archives that would be the storehouse of knowledge of one's "culture" and a testament to the unity and identity of that culture.

As Marianne Hirsch acutely points out, the Assmanns' theoretical apparatus does not "account for the ruptures introduced by collective historical trauma, by war, Holocaust, exile and refugeehood," as it is premised on an assumed continuity among the generations that cannot be easily transposed onto settings marked by catastrophe (Hirsch 2008, 110). To account for such "ruptures and radical breaks," Hirsch

elaborates the notion of "postmemory," which "character-
izes the experience of those who grow up dominated by narratives that preceded their birth, whose own belated stories
are evacuated by the stories of the previous generation
shaped by traumatic events that can be neither understood
nor recreated" (Hirsch 1997, 22). In distinction to the Assmanns' focus on the securing of "identity," Hirsch argues
that postmemory is a "generational *structure* of transmission"
in which photographs—as "living connections" to the
past—play a privileged role in mediation (Hirsch 2008; see
also Hirsch 2012). Yet, like the Assmanns, Hirsch seems to
keep the nested units of individual, family, and public
spheres stable and pregiven when she writes that "the Assmanns' typology explains why and how the postgeneration
could and does work to counteract this loss [of a direct link
to the past]. Postmemorial work . . . strives to reactivate
and reembody more distant social/national and archival/
cultural memorial structures by reinvesting them with resonant individual and familial forms of mediation and aes-
thetic expression" (Hirsch 2008, 111).

    In Hirsch's discussion of postmemory, the reactivation of
more distant memorial structures is undergirded by a particular picture of witnessing as constituted by the institutional
apparatus of testimony. In her discussion of Art Spiegelman's
Maus, for example, Hirsch offers a powerful critique of the
ways in which a dominant male vision of family is superim-
posed onto intimate relations through the "devastating
absence" of the mother, Anja. At the same time, however,
Hirsch herself superimposes the testimonial project back
onto the family when she remarks that in *Maus*, "psychoanalytic and mythic paradigms need to be qualified by the extreme historical circumstances in which they take shape.
Thus, father and son transcend their roles when they become
witness and listener; son and mother become historian and

the object of historical quest" (Hirsch 1997, 35). Here, a witness is constituted in relation to a historical event, which
compels one to take a view over—or up and out of—family.[1]
The family itself remains a relatively stable entity with clearly
defined kinship roles that are known in advance. In this way,
dominant narratives that circulate within the public sphere
in relation to violence—that is, the event as the catastrophic
wound that can be pointed to—are resecured within the site
of the family, understood not as a scene of intimate relations
but as an institution formed in advance. Contrast this work
of postmemory with a child's perspective, in which learning
family—of what "mother," "father," "sister" is and what can
be expected of them—may reveal the ways in which violence
is braided into everyday life, precisely because the child does
not have recourse to a pregiven vocabulary of the historical
event. Thus, rather than transcend intimate relations, the
child is learning what it is to be embedded in them.

Curiously, even as the child comes to be a central figure
within the literature on intergenerational transmission, the
child's puzzling together of the world appears to be continually suppressed in the aspiration to create a more general
theoretical framework—in particular, one that seeks to extend trauma theory to the problem of the intergeneration.
Take Gabriele Schwab's exploration of transgenerational
haunting in relation to war and genocide (Schwab 2010).
Schwab draws on her own childhood memories in which her
mother's loss of her firstborn child haunts their relationship.
Her brother died in infancy during World War II when their
town in Germany was bombed. Schwab recounts how her
mother constantly called her a "changeling, that there was
no way I could be her child. . . . Sometimes she tried to con-
vince my father I was possessed by the devil" (85). It was
only far into adulthood that Schwab could make sense of—
or perhaps make coherent—her mother's words and actions.

On the one hand, Schwab sees her mother as psychotic: "I was already far into my adult life when I figured out that my mother had a form of insanity, a psychotic incapacity to distinguish between reality and fantasy. As a small child, I took her erratic behavior, her unpredictable mood swings, her rages as they came, helpless at first and then defiant" (85). On the other hand, she begins to understand that she was seen as a replacement for the dead firstborn son, which would always be impossible. Schwab relies on the now adult understanding of her mother's "form of insanity" in which the boundary between reality and fantasy is secure. In relying on these adult categories, Schwab seems to create a coherent narrative of the event. But, how might such a recounting be different if she had taken the child's perspective, in which no analytic framework is made available from the start or it is only beginning to take shape through improvisational combinations? How would the relationship of the event and the everyday be rendered if we stayed within the register of the child's voice, who took her mother's "rages as they came"?

In elaborating her theory of haunting, Schwab draws on Nicolas Abraham and Maria Torok's influential theory of transgenerational trauma, a theory that bears an impulse to construct a coherent narrative of the event as a route to healing and recovery (Abraham 1987; Abraham and Torok 1994). Attempting to articulate the transmission of trauma in post-Holocaust psychoanalysis, Abraham and Torok elaborate the notion of the phantom as that unassimilable experience—the "family secret"—that is split off from the self and buried within the unconscious of the first generation. Those unspeakable, unprocessed, and traumatic secrets of the first generation come to haunt the second generation. This haunting occurs because the parent buries the secret in himself, creating "a gap" that is stripped of speech. This gap is incomprehensible and inaccessible to the child and bears "no relation to the patient's own topography but concerns someone else's" (290). Lodged within the unconscious of the child as "bizarre foreign body," the family secret is utterly alien to the second generation and yet productive of effects. Thus, it is not the dead per se that come to haunt the living but rather the "gaps left within us by the secrets of others" (Abraham 1987, 287). As Abraham remarks, *"The phantom which returns to haunt bears witness to the existence of the dead buried within the other"* (291). For Abraham and Torok, analysis can offer a "cure" to the phantom. As Abraham writes, "they [the patients] need only sense, apart from any form of transference, an alliance with the analyst in order to eject a *bizarre foreign body*" (291). Analysis can achieve a gradual fading of the phantom through a mastery of a coherent narrative regarding its effects (see Yassa 2002).[2]

In a review of Abraham and Torok's texts, Christopher Lane astutely points out crucial differences between Abraham and Torok's psychoanalysis and that of Freud and Lacan. Presenting psychoanalysis as a "curing profession," Abraham and Torok "credit the ego with a basic capacity for coherence while representing sexuality (and the drives) as entirely amenable to consciousness" (Lane 1997, 5). This focus on "egoic coherence" and the sidestepping of psychic conflict, Lane argues, is completely at odds with both Freud's and Lacan's much darker visions of psychoanalysis, which Freud considered "interminable" in part because of his realization that "there is something fundamentally incurable in being human" (Lane 1997, 5). In his seminar later published as *The Ethics of Psychoanalysis*, Lacan emphatically rejects the aim of psychoanalysis as the "ideal of psychological harmonization" or the achievement of a "possibility of an untroubled happiness," seeing such aims as making psychoanalysis the "guarantors of the bourgeois dream" (Lacan 1992, 303). Instead, he asserts the tragic dimension of psychoanalysis:

"shouldn't the true termination of analysis . . . in the end confront the one who undergoes it with the reality of the human condition?" (303). For Lacan, this reality of the human condition is anguish connected to distress, "the state in which man is in that relationship to himself which is his own death" (304).

Indeed, this tragic dimension of psychoanalysis indicates a quite different picture of inheritance from the literature on transgenerational haunting, with its emphasis on recovery. As we have seen, Abraham and Torok see the phantom as the parent's "family secret" that becomes embedded within the child's unconscious, thus positing inheritance as a transmission of "family secrets" that come into the consciousness of the adult child through an alliance with the psychoanalyst. Lacan, however, offers a picture of inheritance that is not premised on the transmission of a "gap" held within any one individual but rather is premised on the very entry of the subject into language—that one becomes "subject to" the laws of society through the entry into the symbolic realm and that the unconscious is that "part of concrete discourse qua transindividual, which is not at the subject's disposal in reestablishing the continuity of his conscious discourse" (Lacan 2002, 214). In "The Function and Field of Speech and Language in Psychoanalysis," Lacan describes the realization of the subject through psychoanalysis as the transformation of "empty" to "full speech," in which the psychoanalyst punctuates the individual's "empty speech"—her slips of tongue or parapraxes—while engaging in an interpretation of those "elsewheres" where the truth has already been written—such as in monuments (my body) and "archival documents" (my childhood memories).[3] Through this interaction of the subject's discourse, the analyst's discourse, and the discourse of the Other, full speech emerges, the effect of which is "to reorder the past contingencies by conferring on them the sense of necessities to come, such as they are constituted by the scant freedom through which the subject makes them present" (Lacan 2002, 213). It is through the emergence of full speech that the subject inherits his history—as his unconscious—as it were. And thus, for Lacan, the "analysis can have as its goal only the advent of true speech and the subject's realization of his history in relation to a future" (249).

In his discussion of Antigone, this picture of inheritance as the advent of true speech is explored through the figure of tragedy, one in which inheritance is the movement toward a limit.[4] Antigone bears witness to the uniqueness of being— her brother, condemned as a criminal and denied funerary rites by Creon. Her transgression of the laws of the city, her defiance of Creon, "represents the radical limit that affirms the unique value of his being" (Lacan 1992, 279). This unique value, Lacan argues is "essentially that of language. . . . It is nothing more than the break that the very presence of language inaugurates in the life of man" (279). For Lacan, Antigone is a heroine who engages in a dramatic gesture of transgression, which blinds us with beauty so as to suppress, for us, the "pure and simple desire of death as such. She incarnates that desire" (282).

Interestingly, in the reception of Lacan's discussion of Antigone, it is rarely commented upon that Lacan briefly draws our and his attention to the fact that Antigone is described as "the child" throughout the play: "Have you ever noticed that she is only ever referred to throughout the play with the Greek word ἡ παῖς, which means 'the child'? I say that as a way of coming to the point and of enabling you to focus your eye on the style of the thing" (Lacan 1992, 250). Yet Lacan himself does not elaborate on the significance of the specificity of the child's view in relation to the play's style. In his response to Antigone's lament in which she "evokes the fact that she will never know a conjugal bed, the bond of marriage,

that she will never have any children," Lacan describes Antigone as speaking from the "place she can see it and live it
[her life] in the form of something already lost" (280). He
remarks again on her status as child when he describes how
Antigone's desire shows how the just is unjust, turning the
Chorus on its head: "Nothing is more moving than . . . the
desire that visibly emanates from the eyelids of this admirable
girl" (281). What might be lost or suppressed in resorting to
the great Greek tragedies is that very curiosity and puzzling
of the child, who does not yet have in place the narrative of
the conjugal bed, the bond of marriage, and having children
herself. That is, while Antigone is described by the Chorus
and by Lacan as alternately a child and a girl, we might ask
how the narrative of a heroic gesture in relation to laws that
are already in place, bearing witness to a brother's uniqueness, would differ from the child's learning death.

Consider the poems of Renato Rosaldo in his book *The
Day of Shelly's Death* when he writes through his small son
Sam's voice and describes a scene with Sam and him:

Up a Steep Hill
Dad says Mom's coming,
Gives me a shoulder ride,
once I'm up, says she died.

A low branch. I duck.
Dad's wet back,
muscles like rock.

At least I'm not riding
in yellow backpack,
like a baby.

Dad pants
up a steep hill
to the place

Where an orange
and red tricycle taxi
is waiting.

(Rosaldo 2013, 72)

SAM
He asks me, his father, when
he will get
    a new mother.
        He sits straight, protects
his brother Manny,
pushes my hand
    that seeks to comfort.
        The shoes I chose

Slid off
the crumbling trough.
    He speaks
        My unspoken thought,

Says he wishes
    I had died,
        not her.

(95)

In these poems, we see a child learning death through the
very attention to detail: his dad's wet back, the orange and
red tricycle taxi, the impulse to protect his brother, asking
when he will get a new mother, the anger at the father. There
is no grand narrative that the child's perceptions fit into.
There is no heroic gesture. Rather, the child is simply doing
what he does, putting words and things together, learning
what mother is, learning what father is, learning what brother
is, through learning death and *this* loss. While psychoanalysis

may point to the heroic figure of tragedy, seeing like a child may draw our attention to the ordinary tragedies that are the weave of our lives. Or, to go further, as Stanley Cavell remarks, "In Wittgenstein's diagnosis of the emptying of sense from the philosopher's words (his endless interest in our being led to attempt to mean nonsense), the emptiness of language is not in contest with its fullness, but with its ordinariness or everydayness" (Cavell 2005, 60). In distinction to Lacan's impulse to see full speech in the sublime, we might ask how returning words to the ordinary may present a different route to inheritance and the claiming of a voice.[5]

Ordinary Tragedies

Seeing like a child draws our attention to ordinary tragedies. These tragedies may be the events of war and mass displacement as well as the most uneventful happenings that corrode an everyday life. Indeed, seeing like a child allows us to see the catastrophic in both the event and the uneventful, to see how the event of war and mass displacement may permeate into everyday life and how the uneventful mishaps and afflictions in and of everyday life may also entail catastrophic displacements from home. Inheritance of familial memories of war, then, would not be evidenced in the form of testimony; nor could the impact of the war on the family be recounted in a straightforward empirical account, as if greater historical knowledge of the facts of the war would somehow enable one to do just that.[6] Indeed, the child does not have recourse to historical knowledge in the way that an adult historian might; and perhaps more importantly, because the child is learning the world, she may be only dimly aware of the dangers of the knowledge that she may bear. So, rather than present a coherent narrative of "what happened," a child's learning presents a necessary incoherence, a bewilderment: tidbits of information pulled together from here and there, talk bearing pieces of knowledge whose significance may not be evident, putting together words and actions, tones and gestures as a way of learning what it is to be together with others.

The ethnographic record is littered with children's own attempts to make sense of a world and create a world within contexts of war and poverty. For the most part, we only see these moments in brief glimpses and side glances, detours from a line of sight that focuses on the molding of children by the forces of socialization. There are, however, stunning descriptions that bring these attempts into the center of theorizing the recreation of a world (Das 2015a; Reynolds 2012; Trawick 2007). Through these descriptions, we gain insight not only into children's lives under great pressures but also into how social life comes to be recreated not as a set of stable rules but rather as the child learning words and in so doing "expressing my own desires" (Das 1998). We are also invited to ponder the open question as to how children bear bits of overwhelming adult knowledge that they can barely understand. How does the child learn death and killing in war? In what way does the child's perspective draw our attention to both the ordinary within the scene of war as well as the corrosion of everyday life from within?

In her ethnography on youth in the Liberation Tigers of Tamil Eelam (LTTE), Margaret Trawick describes war, play, and childhood as "supernatural" or transitory states that "coexist with the 'natural' (everyday rule-bound) world, to the extent of being inextricable from it, and necessary to it, as it is to them. But they do not follow the rules of the natural world" (Trawick 2007, 7). In the lives of children in the LTTE, play and war become interchangeable. Yet, while Trawick counterposes "ordinary, stable categories of everyday life" against the "as-if" worlds of war, children, and play, we see in the descriptions of the children she offers that the ordinary is not a cut and dried "rule-bound" world but rather that the ordinary itself is utterly strange, uncanny. Here are some of Trawick's descriptions of her interactions with Vidya (fifteen), Kaveri (eighteen), and Nalini (twelve):

> But Vidya, fifteen years old, speaks as though she would rather be at the front.
> "Aren't you afraid to go into battle?" I ask her.
> "*Chee*—it is play . . ." she says. "A game. On the battlefield we are their equals, and they are ours."
> She asks me what I will do if the army comes. I say, "I guess I will do what everyone else does—what will you do?"
>
> "We will fight," she says proudly.
> "Will you protect me?" I ask. . . .
> "Yes, we will protect you," Vidya says. Then, she looks to Malaimalli for confirmation. "If the army comes, we will protect?" she asks.
> "We will protect," comes the terse answer. (159)

> Vidya is lying down outside under the shade of the *pandal*, and someone says she has a fever. I put my hand on her forehead and ask her what is wrong. She says she has been thinking of too many things.
> "What kinds of things?" I ask.
> "Many things," she says.
> "Family problems?" I ask. The people around smile lightly. "Won't you tell me?" I ask.
> "If I tell you, can you make these troubles go away?" she asks, looking at me with tired, sad eyes.
> "Maybe I can try," I say.
> "My own brother has been sent to Jaffna," she says. "He has been there for twenty-four days." She and others know there is a big battle going on now at

Mangulam. Vidya has two living brothers: one who was in the movement but left to get married, and this brother, who has now been sent to the front. A third brother was killed in battle sometime before. (178)

[Kaveri] is eighteen, she has been in the LTTE for two years, she been in three battles, two of them during Jayasikurui, and she is worried about her dark skin and two missing teeth. When she learns that I am going to town tomorrow, she asks if she can come with me.

"I would take you with me, but if I did, they would kill you," I say, "or at least take you prisoner."

"The brothers go across at night," she says.

"But that is for attacks; they risk their lives: it is dangerous," I say.

"No, they go to visit their families. They wear white shirts."

"If you come across wearing these clothes, the army will shoot you on sight. Wear a dress or something," I say.

"But what about my hair?" she asks.

Her hair is cropped short. It would identify her immediately as a Tiger girl.

"You could wear a wig," suggest the new recruit. They both laugh.

"I want very badly to go to town," says Kaveri. "I want to visit my family."

"Won't they visit you?"

"Yes. But they haven't been to see me recently."

"I can't take you across. You'll be killed," I say.

"It doesn't matter if I die," she says.

"It does matter. You are an important person," I plead. Saying these words make me feel like a youth counselor, inadequate to the task.

"Why am I important?"

"You are *iyakkam*. You are young and brave, and you have a heart made of light." My Tamil fails me. "I now you must fight the army, and in fighting them you may die. But you cannot just throw your life away." (177)

[Nalini] brings me a framed formal photograph of about thirty young Tigre women in uniform, each bearing a rifle and looking serious, arranged in three rows. She points herself out in the picture. . . . She pulls the photograph to her face and kisses the picture. . . . I ask her how many have died. She goes over them one by one: "This one *vīrasā*, this one *vīrasā*, this one alive, this one *vīrasā*," until all of them, including herself ("this one alive") has been accounted for. . . . She produces a fourth wallet-sized photo: a glamorous model in a silk sari with long, silken black hair and pale skin, with a caption advertising some kind of powder. "This is my mother," says Nalini. And then she says, "This is you."

She turns the picture over, takes a pen, and says, "I will write your name."

"Don't write my name there," I say. "It's not my picture."

But she ignores me and spells out the Tamil letters *pa-ki-ya-n-ti* (Peggy Auntie) on the back of the model's photograph. "Is that right?" she asks. (182–83)

In these scenes, we see girls bearing bits and pieces of knowledge of the adult world of war, and, through the interactions with others, showing what they somewhat know and what they are struggling to understand, and at times showing the anthropologist her own failures of knowledge. Thus, Nalini points out, as if it were just a recounting of small events, "This one dead, this one alive," while weaving a story of her mother as a glamourous model and simultaneously projecting Trawick as an as-if mother to her. We see Vidya at first pronouncing proudly that she will fight, then asking tentatively, "We will protect?" Later, we hear Vidya's anxieties surrounding her brother who was sent to the front, and we might feel a tinge of irony in her voice when she asks Trawick, "If I tell you, you will make these troubles go away?" as if it were that simple. We see Kaveri missing her family and perhaps hear in her words a desire to leave the LTTE, a desire that must remain unvoiced. At the same time, she recoils Trawick's insistence that she remain in the camp for fear of being killed back on Trawick—"It doesn't matter if I die. . . . Why am I important?"—as if to show to Trawick that an insistence that she remain alive may come at the cost of her life with others. Here, while Trawick remarks, "My Tamil fails me," we might instead see a difficulty in listening to or absorbing this reality.

Trawick's descriptions show us how the categories of child and adult are unstable and how learning death and learning killing happens in the concrete interactions with other children and adults, where they are not only stealing bits of knowledge but testing what is known. As Veena Das shows in her ethnography in low-income neighborhoods in Delhi, "children can become ventriloquists voicing the desires of adults; and they can invest themselves in role performances that cast them as as-if adults" (Das 2015a, 60). She describes the case of Mukesh, an eight-year-old boy, who was simultaneously the caretaker and guardian of his ailing mother as well as the child who bore overwhelming knowledge that his father might be abandoning his mother for another woman. Mukesh gets bits and pieces of information that come his way, "guessing at what are the consequences of adult desires, such as that of his father for another woman" (65). In staying true to those bits and pieces, Das shows us how a child invents himself and is marked through catastrophe—not from war but from the everyday deprivations and the corrosions from within the politics of the family. In this context of illness and death, the "ordinary" is strange or uncanny, in which a "complex layering of family relations with the institutions of the state came to define the quotidian in the overall context of poverty and deprivation and created the sense of reality as precarious" (61).

The idea of the child as "hovering around the social, stealing rather than formally learning language and then slowly putting the world together as his or her own" offers a profound insight into writing the inheritance of familial memories of war (Das 2015a, 61). For it asks us not to achieve "recovery" from a transgenerational haunting or boldly transgress a limit but rather asks us to recover a child's bewilderment such that we can perceive ordinary tragedy—those "small, recurring, repetitive crises almost woven into everyday life itself"—such that we might also come to perceive the texture of reinhabiting that everyday life (Das 2020, 16). Paola Marrati describes this recovery or reanimation of the child's bewilderment as the condition of "having been a child": "a condition that none of us—no matter how different our happy or unhappy stories may be—can ever overcome, grow out of. 'Having been a child' is not a fact from the past that we may indifferently recall or forget, but rather an internal aspect of our existence that will last as long as we do" (Marrati 2011, 957). Marrati sees here an inherent connection between childhood and philosophy, that childhood events have to do with the "life of the mind" and are "intellectually powerful." She draws our attention to a citation from Stanley Cavell's autobiography *Little Did I Know*:

Socrates invents a world of philosophy by confronting
assertions of people who claim to know what the world
is, already producing as it were unthoughtful philosophy,
so that the philosopher's immediate task is to reveal
their bewilderment to them and get them to stop.
Whereas thoughtful responses to childhood's reflections are not to lead them to self-repudiation but to
help them go on, to further their exploratory responses,
as if listening for orienting echoes of their assertions as
they wonder what the world is, what its things and
persons are to expect of each other. Blocking adult
certainties philosophically is a way of asking that
childhood be remembered; drawing out childhood
uncertainties is a matter of suggesting that adulthood
not be sought too quickly. (Cavell 2010, 461–62)

In remembering childhood, I try to reanimate that bewilderment at the most seemingly mundane happenings of a
domestic life and yet show how this domestic life in this way
bears the impulses of death and life within it: the reinhabitation of life marked by war, as well as the undoings
of that reinhabitation by illness. Attempts to interrogate
the anthropologist's own situation within family histories
have most often been discussed in relation to the genres of
autoethnography (Bourgois 2005; Kidron 2009; Panourgiá
1995; Waterston and Rylko-Bauer 2006). Yet, one senses in
the genres of autoethnography (Panourgiá 1995) and "intimate ethnography" (Waterston and Rylko-Bauer 2006), as
well as the more recent conversations between biography and
ethnography (Carsten 2018; Carsten, Day, and Stafford 2018),
the tension between the intellectual apparatus of professional
anthropology that seeks to place and identify relevant "personal" details into a historical grid and the fluttering shadows of the subjective experience of violence that comes to

color the child's world.[7] *Seeing Like a Child* attempts to take this subjective experience as ethnographic material in its own right, asking how we can learn from this material, rather than overwrite it with stable adult categories such as "mental illness," "history," and "victim." In this way, I also explore alignments of anthropology and autobiography.

Anthropology and Autobiography

In opening her lecture on ordinary ethics, Veena Das describes a picture of thought as a movement of descent: "The everyday . . . is taut with moments of world-making and world-annihilating encounters that could unfold in a few seconds or over the course of a life" (Das 2015b, 54). Das returns to Manjit, a woman who had been abducted during the Partition and then rescued by the Indian Army, describing Manjit's "work of repair and containment of violence" as a "spiritual exercise" (see Das 2007). While philosopher Pierre Hadot describes "spiritual exercises" as growing from within a history of (Western) philosophy, the spiritual exercises he describes are those that make the philosopher transcend everyday life through the "view from above and the flight of the soul" or "the viewpoint of the gods" (Hadot 1995, 239). By calling Manjit's patient biding of time amid poisonous kinship relations a "spiritual exercise," Das is "trying to wrest the very expression away from the profundity of philosophy to the small disciplines that ordinary people perform in their everyday lives to hold life together as the 'natural' expression of ethics" (Das 2015b, 54). This picture of thought as descent brings the method of ethnography as a "mode of critical patience" into close proximity with biography. Ordinary ethics "binds the ethnographer and the people she finds in mutually discovering what it is to find a voice in one's history" (Das 2015b, 89). In this binding, the method of ethnography itself is learned from concrete flesh-and-blood others in the rough and tumble of everyday life. What it is to be an anthropologist, and what constitutes anthropological knowledge, is bound up with this learning. At the same time, being an anthropologist comes to suffuse what it is to live our lives and to write lives that we could claim as "ours." Ethnography permeates biography in terms of experience that marks us and in terms of a method that becomes a way of being in the world (see also Carsten, Day, and Stafford 2018).

There appears to be a deep gulf between the intimacy described here and a fallback notion of "self-reflexivity" that circulates in professional anthropology. In the efforts to critique epistemological underpinnings of knowledge production, the "I" is often taken as a standpoint, a particular ready-made perch from which the anthropologist, in supreme efforts at self-consciousness, critiques his positionality within a grid of unequal relations (Clifford and Marcus 1986; for a critique, see Strathern 1987).[8] Alternatively, attempts at "self-revelation" that seek to bring "the personal" into ethnography have a tendency to take rather unproblematically what it is to write in the first person. The first person is assumed to be a fully formed identity and the problem of writing this "self" is seen as a problem that has to do with professional norms, our own courage to be "vulnerable," and writerly skill (Behar 2014). Yet, rather than assume the "I" as one standpoint among others that are ready-made or as fully formed identities, the "I" can be taken as an achievement. It marks the struggle of finding a voice within and through a life in which we are mutually absorbed with others.

One can see this struggle in some of the most perceptive writing that seeks to imprint ethnography and biography on each other. In his memoir *The Accidental Anthropologist*, anthropologist Michael Jackson writes of the tensions of inhabiting both the academic conventions of professional

anthropology and the life-sustaining nature of fieldwork and
writing poetry (Jackson 2006). He comes to see these struggles as a tension between science and art. Yet, his memoir is
also marked here and there by his wife Pauline's long struggle with cancer: first with Hodgkin's lymphoma and then
cervical cancer, to which she succumbs. In one scene, he
describes the tension between science and art through the
sense of estrangement that permeates his relationship to his
old friends. Yet, in the same breath, Pauline's illness appears,
"We [Jackson and his old friend] talked about writing, but it
was clear that we were headed in very different directions.
While Harry was entranced by Márquez and magical real-
ism, I distrusted fantasy. Dealing with Pauline's illness and
working doggedly on my African material, I was guided by
Cendrars' dictum that one must write as one eats or breaths"
(197). It emerges again when Jackson draws a parallel between
the tension between art and science and Pauline's impatience
with medical treatment.

These small glimpses of Pauline's illness as it colored the
domestic seem be tamed, in some way, by turning to writing and writers. Jackson describes the circumstances surrounding the death of writer Antoine de Saint-Exupéry to
ask if we do not all "improvise with what we remember of
the past, that no one, not even the most conscientious scholar,
lives his or her life faithfully recapitulating what has been said
and done" (Jackson 2006, 206). He turns to Blaise Cendrars's
writings to suggest that perhaps the pain of Pauline's illness
and her death may simply not be that which can be put in
writing, shared with an anonymous public: "There are certain events and experiences of which we choose not to
speak. Not because they hold us in thrall, stilling the tongue.
Nor because we fear they might reveal our flaws or frailty.
Still less because we feel our words can never do them justice. Silence is sometimes the only way that we can honour

the ineffability and privacy of certain experiences" (209). Yet, Pauline's illness and her death return again with Jackson tersely recounting her diagnosis of cervical cancer and her refusal of standard treatment. He indicates what must have been heart-wrenching conditions surrounding Pauline's death: living in the same place where they had lived for so many years, Jackson's own need to leave that place but his daughter Heidi's need for stability; Jackson's homeschooling of his daughter after her mother dies; finally, their move to Canberra "to start over." There, in Canberra, writing seems to provide some way to escape from what seems to be a menace of the domestic itself:

> But, it troubled me deeply that I could not conjure her image in my mind's eye, could no longer hear her voice, or recall the touch of her hand, nor the smell and contours of her body. At times I struggled against the silence and emptiness; at times I submitted to it, not wanting to fill it with my desperate imaginings, or the noise of my own grieving. And so I dreamt. Strange dreams in which she would appear to me contorted and monstrous. But then, that winter, night after night I woke from dreams that were adrift in words. Words I scribbled half asleep on scraps of paper by my bedside, and typed up in the mornings after Heidi left for school. (213)

This writing transforms into a poem that, in its form, bears the imprint of both Blaise Cendrars's poetry as well as the "secret book" on the life of Mary Magdalene that Cendrars had been working on but never published. While the repeated turn to writing and the figure of the writer provides some salve for a menacing domestic, it also seems that Jackson's writing cannot but be entangled with that domestic. Would dwelling in that domestic have offered a picture of healing and reinhabitation, different from the salve of writing as an imagined exit from the everyday?

In the movement of descent, we see that the struggle of finding a voice appears in the most quotidian moments in one's life, moments that lay right before our eyes yet somehow remain unseen. Writing through the first person, then, is a labor on ourselves, in which we write those quotidian moments and see their significance and relevance for ourselves. Philosopher Sandra Laugier helps us articulate these thoughts. In her remarks on Stanley Cavell's autobiography *Little Did I Know,* Laugier describes the significance of Cavell's teaching as "teaching each of us . . . what *importance* is, that is, what is important to us (to me, to you). In other words: he teaches us how to learn from ourselves what is important to us" (Laugier 2011, 996). In particular, Cavell describes "unseen importance of moments in a life." It is not only the accidents and swerves from birth to death that mark turning points in one's life but also the fact that the significance of such accidents and swerves can be missed. As Laugier remarks, *"Little Did I Know* describes both this kind of terror (connected to the terror of an abusive father figure) of missing what matters, and the methods (attention to human conversations, reading of expression) found to overcome it, alternative ways of finding, and expressing importance" (998).

This learning "from ourselves what is important to us" is enmeshed in relations to concrete others, the "you" who shares a world with me. Our existence is staked in them. Writing in the first person as a movement of descent, then, has the addressee as the second person, with whom I inhabit a world and who I hope will be able to receive my words. These are family, friends, colleagues, readers of this book. Yet, the third person also circulates around and through me, such as the dominant narratives of war and violence that

I engage in this book as well as in others. In this braiding of the second and third person into the first person, we see the instability of the self rather than its narrative unity. Multiple voices live within us, and it can be extremely difficult to really know when our words are spoken as ghosts and, alternatively, if and how the words of the other give a pulse to lives that we claim as our own. Perhaps I might say that far from being authorial or authoritative, this writing is continually asking what the conditions are for saying "I"—that is, what are the conditions in which we are challenged to have a deeper sense of ourselves and to be able to find a voice that we claim as our own.

The Korean War and the War at Home

This book is a response to my mother and father, both of whom were displaced from the North of Korea during the war. It asks what a body of writing itself could be between the generations. That is, can this body of writing give birth to a mother (my own and myself) and a daughter (myself and my daughter)?

The Korean War was the first "hot war" of the Cold War, in which mass mechanical death and displacement was wrought on a people in the name of a bipolar world (Cumings 2011; Kwon 2010). Millions of people died during the war. Millions of others were displaced, their kinship relations rendered fugitive in a context of virulent anticommunist violence in South Korea and anticommunist repression in the United States. As anthropologist Heonik Kwon remarks, the Korean War was not a single war but rather a "combination of several different kinds of wars": it was a civil war in which two different postcolonial forces sought to assert their vision of national independence from the colonial apparatus of imperial Japan; an international war divided along ideological lines; and a war waged over who could authorize the political subject in Korea (see also M. Kim 2019; Kwon 2015, 78). But, as Kwon points out, there was also another war, "the other Korean War," which was a "war against the civilian population": "the war was centrally about the struggle for survival by unarmed civilians against the generalized, indiscriminate violence perpetrated by the armed political forces on all sides" (Kwon 2015, 78).[9]

While war broke out in June 1950, preceding this "official start," anticommunist violence was already being waged in the South. From 1947, Jeju Island, an island at the southern tip of South Korea, was a site of a counterinsurgency war that led to the death of one-tenth of the island's population, approximately thirty thousand people. This counterinsurgency war is referred to as the Jeju 4.3 Incident. On April 3, 1948, a communist-led uprising to protest the United States' military occupation and its aim to create an anticommunist state in South Korea was met with brutal military counterinsurgency campaigns carried out by South Korean police but with the support of the United States Army Military Government in Korea (USAMGIK; Hwang 2016).

On the mainland, the commencement of war went hand in hand with the extremely efficient mass killing of those suspected of being communist sympathizers. In 1949, the South Korean regime led by Syngman Rhee and supported by the USAMGIK established the National Guidance Alliance, a policy and apparatus to root out and eradicate South Korean communists. As historian Su-Kyoung Hwang describes, the models for the National Guidance Alliance were drawn from the Japanese police state. In Japan, *tenkō*, or "conversion," was consolidated into the Peace Preservation Law in 1925. The law facilitated the mass arrest of Japanese communists, show trials with the aim of public recantation, and their long-term surveillance at the community level.

While in Japan, tenkō "resulted in only one execution out of all of the mass arrests, the Alliance led to the deaths of hundreds and thousands in 1950" (Hwang 2016, 89). In South Korea, the National Guidance Alliance was conceived under the fascist principle of *ilmin*, or "one people," that premised the nation as an ethnically homogeneous organic entity. The Alliance relied on a highly organized infrastructure that connected a central headquarters in Seoul with a web of regional offices in the provinces. Recruitment into the Alliance went all the way to the village level. At the outbreak of the war, this highly organized surveillance web established the conditions for mass executions, as Hwang remarks: "The war did not disband the Alliance but destroyed it. Most executions took place in the first six months of the war outside of metropolitan Seoul. The highly systematic organization of the Alliance made the remobilization of members swift and easy" (102). It is estimated that around two hundred thousand people were killed in the pogroms of 1950.

In South Korea, anticommunist violence intensified, and was intensified by, a police state. As anthropologist Heonik Kwon acutely observes in his work on Korean War mass graves, violence was directed not only at individual bodies but also at the relations through which individuality could be claimed. This apparatus of punishment and surveillance of kinship, called *yŏnjwaje*, or "guilt by association," formed a "shadowy legal and political rule" that continued long into the postwar years, with discriminatory effects outlasting its official abolishment in 1980 (Kwon 2015, 84).

Yŏnjwaje both intensified and destroyed kinship relatedness. It was premised on kinship relations: it used them in the enactment of state terror and the securing of a virulent anticommunist police state. At the same time, yŏnjwaje made kinship the site of profound existential violations. Those who had relatives killed in the name of anticommunism, those who were related to those accused of being a communist sympathizer, and those who had relatives who returned to the North during the tumultuous period of the war and were in the condition of "separated family" were put into an impossible situation: either they renounced their kinship relation to the accused individual and became "good citizens" or they faced punishment themselves. As a result, people who found themselves in this predicament had to make up false death records for those who had been killed in mass executions, or they simply annulled them from genealogy; those who had relatives in the North conducted funerary rites for the living, a profound moral violation that excised living kin from kinship (see N. Kim 2017; Koh 2018). In describing the impossible situation in which families found themselves, Kwon turns to Hegel and his elaboration of the figure of Antigone, who is "torn between the obligation to bury her war-dead brothers according to 'the divine law' of kinship on the one hand and, on the other, the reality of 'the human law' of the state, which prohibited her from giving burial to the enemies of the state" (Kwon 2015, 88). That is, relatedness itself was suspended within the contradiction between the norms of kinship and subjection to the state.

In contemporary South Korea, the commemoration of the dead has become an important site for addressing this state persecution of relatedness. Anthropologist Seong Nae Kim shows how public memory of Jeju 4.3 is mediated through families' agonizing consent to have their relatives' remains dispersed between the family cemetery, the public ossuary, and public shrine, as testament to the national project of transitional justice (S. N. Kim 2019). Further, anthropologist Sungman Koh describes how the re-establishment of genealogy—or the transformation of the missing dead and their ghosts to ancestors—is intertwined with the ability of relatives to secure recognition as official victims. The state's recognition of victimhood removes the stain of communism from the web of kinship but resecures the importance of the state in defining relatedness (Koh 2018). At the same time, Koh also shows how Confucian norms that undergird patriarchy are drawn upon and experimented with as relatives piece together genealogical kinship that was fractured through the violent deaths of their kin.

While the reconstitution of kinship relatedness has emerged as a key site for the project of transitional justice, the state's imprint on kinship is powerfully seen in the anthropological record: that is, ancestral rites resecure a normative kinship based on filial piety and the re-establishment of the patriline. As Nan Kim points out, "the significance of family as a site of post-conflict reconciliation in South Korea is complicated by a lengthy history of moralizing state appropriations of filial piety discourses" (N. Kim 2017, 174). In her remarkable ethnography of the reunions of separated families, those families separated by the partition of North and South, Kim describes how separated families under the dictatorship of Park Chung Hee were compelled to sever their kinship relations with their relatives in the North. Yet, in the wake of the Asian Financial Crisis and South Korea's economic need for North Korea, and under the Kim Dae-jung administration's Sunshine Policy, these same families were held up as the beacon of reconciliation: "Through this unexpected reversal of fortunes, these families emerged in August 2000 as the visible and embodied link between two inverse agendas by different governments in South Korea's modern past—the consolidation of the anticommunist state under Park Chung Hee and the pursuit of reconciliation with the North during the Sunshine Era under Kim Dae-jung" (182). As Kim shows, in the mediatized reunions in South Korea, certain kinship relationship gained traction in the public sphere—that of mothers and sons—while other relationships—such as the relations of separated husbands and wives—were suppressed. Such privileging of normative kinship roles reveals how patriarchy, memory, and nationalism are intertwined.

Feminist scholars have sought to broaden the descriptive range of experiences of war by bringing into focus what remains unseen and unheard amid this entanglement of kinship and the state. In relation to the Jeju 4.3 Incident, for example, Eun-Shil Kim explores how a focus on the official discourse around victimhood and memorialization tends to create a blindness to women's embodied suffering (E. Kim 2017), while Seong Nae Kim describes the ways in which the religious practices of women have inherited tabooed memories and the wounds of the dead (S. N. Kim 2013). In this work, the figure of Antigone is perhaps one less posed between the "law of kinship" and the "law of the state" than the figure who acknowledges the wounds to relatedness that cannot be subsumed into a picture of normative kinship.[10]

But what if the perspective of the child were taken, rather than adults who mourn? How does a child learn death, loss, and kinship? In a fascinating study of the memory of the Korean War in literature, literary scholar Seunghei Clara Hong discusses Oh Junghee's novella *Garden of Childhood*, a story told through the eyes of a seven-year-old girl and in her words, but as recollected by the girl as an adult who is remembering scenes of family in the midst of the Korean War (Oh [1981] 2017). The family has fled from Seoul and are in a small village in the South. The father was drafted into the South Korean army as they were fleeing south. The mother is working in a bar in the village and is engaged in sex for money to support the household in the absence of the father. The oldest brother, in the absence of the father, attempts to assert himself as the patriarch, but he is constantly failing, as the mother is the one who sustains the household economy. The scene of family here is not one of safety or sentimentality but is marked by the corrosive force of poverty, rage, spitefulness, and malaise. Men in the home are violent; women trade their bodies. Thus, kinship does not appear as a redemptive force but rather as the scene where cruelty is intertwined with the labor of reinhabiting everyday life under the pressures of war. The Korean War here is a war at home.

Let me focus on Hong's discussion of names in the story. Hong draws our attention to the fact that there are no proper names in the story, only the use of kinship terms: Grandmother, Mother, Father, Oldest Brother, Older Sister, Older Brother, Baby Brother. The narrator "I" (or *na*) is never referred to by a proper name or a kinship term, rather she is referred to by a host of nicknames, but primarily called Yellow Eyes (*norangnuni*) by her family. Yellow Eyes, the protagonist, is an "I" without a proper name, one that would enmesh her within genealogical kinship. Yet, this namelessness—the "I" without biography—becomes the site of memory as "self-invention" in which ordinary details such as the stickiness of a persimmon or the sweetness of candy are put up against the impulse to write a totalizing history of the Korean War. As Hong writes, "in the absence of a patrilineal name the body breaks down—she is Yellow Eyes. This, in turn, makes possible the emergence of an altogether different bodily coherence. As Norangnuni, the narrator has a name that is part of a body from which all other bodies may be re-imagined, re-collected, re-membered" (Hong 2009, 138). Memory from this site of namelessness is unsettling. There is no promise of reconstruction, no biography to be made, no resecuring of kinship with nation. As Norangnuni says, "I wonder if the real me remains a broken feeling within the sorrowful recollections of a distant fragment of memory. Like father. For aren't all my memories

just a product of my imagining a far distant dream?" (139).
Seeing like a child invites us to witness this dream.

§

My writing is marked by the history of war and yet, as I describe in Part I, when I enter into the inside of my childhood memories, the subjective experience of history is simply not available to me. Instead, I explore how an inheritance of the Korean War might be possible if Korea and Korean are inherited in myth, in fragment, and in ordinary tragedies. My writing moves through four themes. Part I, "Loss and Awakenings," describes affliction within the domestic as a route into the child's inheritance of catastrophe. Part II, "A Future in Kinship, a Future in Language," describes my learning of Korean, which is part and parcel of the learning of kinship separated and suppressed within my family. Part III, "The Kids," describes siblings' talk and relations to explore how the sibling relation may present a different picture of inheritance. Part IV, "Mother Tongue," returns once again to affliction and war, exploring a picture of care between the generations.

PART I
Loss and Awakenings

I'm a small girl wandering around my mother and father's bedroom. I loved to look into my mother's dresser, a treasure trove of mysteries. Where did we come from? Inside the top drawer of Mom's dresser is a large red-brown lacquered hexagon box with mother-of-pearl inlay. The box has a pearl necklace, a pair of white satin gloves with white fur trim, a similar pair in black, and scarves, brooches, and black with mother-of-pearl clip-on earrings. In the bottom drawer, Mom has her hanbok, turquoise silk with patterns. I tell the other kids at school that my mom was a princess who escaped from her country, Korea. So that is how we all ended up here in New Mexico. Someday Mom will go back to claim her fortune as a princess. So actually, we are incredibly rich.

Forebodings

When my twin brother and I were three years old, my sister four, and my older brother nine, we moved from Pennsylvania, where my father had worked as a college professor in physics and my mother as a researcher at a cancer institute, to Los Alamos, New Mexico. They both began jobs as research scientists at Los Alamos National Laboratory—or, as everyone in town calls it, "The Lab"—the town where the atomic bomb was made, a "company town" that only exists because of a national defense laboratory. My father has often said to me that moving to Los Alamos was the biggest mistake he has ever made in his life. Had he known what would happen to our family here, he would have taken the job he was offered in Brazil, as a professor at the University of São Paulo. When my twin brother and I were eleven years old, my mother had a stroke, followed by a catastrophic rise in brain pressure. She sustained massive brain damage and remained in a vegetative state for nearly a decade afterward. For several years, we took care of our mother in our home.

My memories of our first years in Los Alamos are the little flashes here and there that a small child has—disconnected moments, particular tones of voice, smells, an image. My siblings and I are with our mom and dad in a strange house. The kitchen counter has two barstools. There's a dog that is taller than me. Dad is opening and closing a kitchen cabinet. A woman offers us juice. She calls my mom "Joan." I ask Mom as we are leaving, "Why doesn't she call you 'Chung'?" She pinches me on the arm. We move into a house in Los Alamos. We move again to another house in the suburb called White Rock. The family who is moving out is called "The Bloods." Their name is on the mailbox. The children, older than us, are showing me and my twin brother large green grasshoppers in the backyard, telling us that if you squish them, you can eat their insides, because they are made of macaroni and cheese. I look up from the concrete patio where I am squatting next to a muddy sandbox and see my father's face through the backyard screen door.

He yells at us to get out of the mud, even though we are not in it.

A terrible feeling of impending doom began to take shape in my small body as we were living in that house, the house where my father still lives. I do not know when I began to pray to God for world peace, but I began to do so every night before I fell asleep in the bed that I shared with my sister. PBS is airing the made-for-television movie *Threads* on nuclear annihilation. My father is lying on the couch, watching. He yells at my siblings and me to go to our rooms. My mother takes us into my twin brother's bedroom to listen to classical music and play games, but not before I see images: a woman is standing in a building, the floors above her are torn off, she's screaming, her skeleton briefly flashing in white, surrounded by red heat, and then dissipating into ashes. I hold this image with me, in terror. On nights afterward, I lie on the couch in the family room, cover myself with a blanket and cry.

In elementary school, our class makes a field trip to the Bradbury Science Museum. We sit in a small theater on black carpeted steps, watching a documentary on Los Alamos. The footage is in black and white. Shirtless young boys run around the Fuller Lodge, a private ranch school that was transformed into a mess hall for the Manhattan Project; trucks getting stuck in the mud as they make their way up the hill to Los Alamos; Einstein walking in the woods. It ends with the mushroom cloud and a close up of Robert Oppenheimer's face. He says he is quoting from the Bhagavad Gita, "Now I am become Death, the destroyer of all worlds." The teacher says that Los Alamos would be the first place to be bombed in a nuclear war. The earth would be covered in ashes that would coat the ground like snow. She's showing us a cartoon book: a man in a grey winter jacket, looking down as ashes fall. The sky is dark. She says that we have a bomb shelter underneath the community center where the town would be able to survive. "Please, God, don't let there be nuclear war," I say to myself. In *The Monitor* (the local newspaper) there is a photo of a little girl holding a flower, protected from nuclear warheads by a dome, an anti-ballistic missile system.

Our father watches the television program *World at War* on PBS. He lies on the couch, hands behind his head, silent. From the TV: black-and-white footage of airplanes dropping bombs and explosions on land, military ships firing artillery, men in fatigues running over sand dunes. A squeaky radio announcer voice listing names of battles and their dates. I don't know what war is being narrated. The images, that voice, and our father's heavy presence draw me in and out of our bustling household: the sound of our mother chopping vegetables; my older brother playing a Lionel Ritchie album; my siblings and I reading stories to each other and our mother that we had written with the babysitter.

§

My father sometimes works from home at night and on weekends. He calls into a supercomputer from our house, using a machine that looks like a typewriter but with two suction cups on top. He dials from our rotary home phone, plugs the phone into the suction cup machine, and it starts to spurt out numbers on what looks like receipt paper, which he reads through his thick reading glasses. There's the smell of ink and rubber. He goes to conferences, but I only remember his returns. His suitcase is open in the living room. He gives us presents. I get a blue and white striped dress that I insist on wearing to preschool the next day. At some point, though, he stops bringing home the typewriter with suction cups and stops returning from trips. As we talk on the phone, I tell my sister that I don't remember when our father was fired from The Lab, our conversation veering into our childhoods as it often does, as we deal with our father's difficult care situation today. He has uncontrolled diabetes, early dementia, clinical depression—these categories and our dark humor are ways of taming the madness. She remembers him at home all the time, smoking cigarettes in the garage.

As a small child, I often snuck into my mother and father's bed to sleep in between them. My mother is quietly and angrily scolding my father in Korean. She reaches over my body and gives him a jab, and then gives him another jab. My father lifts me up out of the middle of the bed and puts me to the side. My mother continues to scold him. My father is talking back to her harshly in hushed tones. He places me back in between them. It's quiet and I am drifting to sleep, but then my father gets up from the bed with a "Tch-hhh," grabbing his pillow and leaving the room. I snuggle into my mother. At some point, though, my mother is sleeping alone in the bedroom, and my father is sleeping in the family room, with the TV constantly on. There is a clock on my mother's dresser now. It's metal and has red and green buttons. The alarm would ring, she would get up, and go back to the lab, where she was running experiments. She is falling asleep at the dinner table. One of her eyes is completely bloodshot. She comes home with stitches on her thumb that she tries to hide from us by wrapping it in a paper towel. I point to it as she cooks. She tells me that it was an accident in the lab.

My mother's younger sister, Auntie Young, comes to visit us from Korea. We're waiting at the gate, watching her come down the steps of the plane. Her hair is in a bob. She is wearing a long blue skirt and a yellow and white plaid shirt. I am standing on tiptoe to see over the waist-high bar that runs across the floor-to-ceiling windows of the Albuquerque airport. She has cool hands like my mother, the kind of hands that cool down a mosquito bite or a feverish head when one

is ill. Auntie Young brings us lots of gifts: nightgowns, long
underwear, washcloths, a wood-carved set of a mother pig
and six piglets, which I have today in our house in Baltimore.
Our mother spends time with Auntie Young alone in my
twin brother's room. My sister tells me her memories of Auntie Young's visit: that when Auntie Young was packing her
bags, she told Alyse that our mother was not doing well and
that we need to take care of her.

Separated Family

When my siblings and I are around eight or nine years old,
my mother organizes a Korean cultural event for the Presbyterian church that she brings my sister, my twin brother,
and me to every Sunday. She is cooking all weekend, making kimbap, pajeon, kalbi, japchae . . . She makes us practice
"Arirang" on our violins and on the piano while she sings.
We painstakingly make the 태극기 (South Korean flag) from
small dowel rods and white cloth, which are paired with US
flags and placed on each table. She is wearing her turquoise
hanbok. My father does not come to the event. It is not
surprising to us. He hates church. Reverend Parker is tall,
stone-faced, with powder-white skin. He wears dark glasses.
Dressed in a white robe with a blue, green, and purple sash
draped over his shoulders, he walks slowly into the hall as
the organ plays and he takes his place at the pulpit. My
mother sings in the choir. After his sermon, Reverend Parker
beckons the children in the congregation to sit on the steps
of the pulpit where he tells a moral story with characters from
the Bible. The soft voice he takes on with us battles with the
severe lines in his face. The one time I remember my father
coming to church with us, he sat in the back in a long, tan
coat, leaning his chair against the wall, fast asleep. Afterward,
he takes us to the soccer field next to the church and glee-

fully says, "Let's race!" We run with abandon on the field,
getting grass stains on our Sunday clothes. I feel my mother's
eyes on my back.

It would only dawn on me much later that my father did
not attend the cultural event not only because he hated
church but also because he hated Korea—that is, the fact of
it being a North and a South, which at the time and also
today seems to be the conditions of intelligibility for being
Korean at all. Both my parents fled from North to South during the war. My mother's family comes from Chŏngju (정주) in
North Pyongan Province, on the western side of the Korean
peninsula. Positioned in intellectual and trade routes between China and Seoul, Chŏngju was known as a city of
scholars, writers, and artists. When I meet my aunt, she names
famous figures to me: the poet Kim Sowŏl, the painter Lee
Jung-seob, the philosopher Ham Seok Heon. My mother's
father fled South after the nuclear catastrophe of Hiroshima,
leaving his family behind. My grandmother, my mother and
her sisters and brothers, later fled South as the war broke out.
My mother came to the United States in 1953 sponsored by
an American family. My father, however, comes from the
rugged terrain of Sinheung (신흥) in South Hamgyŏng Province on the eastern side of the peninsula. This is what my
father's older brother's daughter, Sung Sook, tells me, though
my father has always said that he comes from Hamheung,
just south of Sinheung. My father's family is a "separated
family" (이산 가족). My father, his older brother, and his eldest sister were separated from their mother, second eldest
sister, and younger brother when the thirty-eighth parallel
was hardened with the occupation of the two Koreas. My
father and mother met when they were doctoral students at
the University of Massachusetts. As a child, the knowledge
of my family's status as a "separated family" and the displacements of my father's and my mother's families, however, was

not available to me in a chronologically ordered narrative. Today, through conversations with my cousins, I have been able to partially reconstruct some of the movements of my parents, though my cousins' knowledge of our families in the North has a similar patchy, dispersed quality. Like them, my siblings and I gained a fuzzy, shifting knowledge of the existence of kin by picking up little bits and pieces from the flow of everyday life: the fact that my mother's sisters visited us, so we knew we had aunts; a phone call when my father learned of his brother's death, so we learned our father had a brother.

Some years ago, my sister, twin brother, and I fly my father out to San Francisco, where my sister and twin brother live, for a short trip. We take him to the Asian Art Museum to see the special exhibit on mother-of-pearl lacquerware from Korea. On the wall, there is a map of the Korean peninsula. My sister asks our father to recount how he fled from North to South. He traces the movements with his hand, from Hungnam port in the North to Busan in the South by boat, from Busan to Seoul on top of a cargo train, enduring the terrible cold to arrive at his sister and sister's husband's house, from Incheon back to Busan by boat in a mass displacement from Seoul. "Those were terrible times," he says. I think he is referring to the movements he had just traced. But he goes on, "We were students wearing white bands on our heads, shouting, our arms raised. I was running over the rooftops with my friend. I turn around and I see him getting shot. How could they mow down hundreds of students just like that? Only machines could do that." He is speaking of the April 19 Revolution in 1960 when hundreds of thousands of students took to the streets to protest the rule of Syngman Rhee. These protests led to Rhee's resignation, but not before a massacre of those student protestors. I discover then that my father had participated in the protests.

§

I have been working on creating conditions in which I can
undertake anthropological research in Korea. First, on a history of displacement in my own family, and second, on a
project on suicide in old age, in the context of political economic transformation, urban migration, and the changing
status of parents within kinship. The work involved in shifting from my long-term fieldwork in Santiago, Chile—where
I explored how state violence and economic precarity is
absorbed into everyday life in low-income neighborhoods—
has been enormous. But I find that blood is again flowing
through the veins of my reading, teaching, and writing. I'm
invited into new but familiar sets of conversations with new
and old friends who are embedded with me in a shared in-
tegument. They describe how the cold war and the Korean
War are at the heart of kinship relations (see Kwon 2010;
Kwon 2020). These conversations prod me to consider not
only how life in kinship is embedded within a historical context but also how that history is subjectively experienced.
Yet, when I enter into the inside of my childhood memories,
I'm accompanied by a strange feeling that our family resided
outside of historical time; that somehow the subjective experience of historical time was simply not available to us.

With our mother's illness and death, we may have lost a
possibility of claiming a place in South Korea through kinship
and through the identification with the nation-building
diaspora. In my childhood memories, Korea emerges in bits
and pieces, in the origin myths I hold onto (like my mother
is a princess), in the medicines we give our mother, in phone
calls, and in my father's fragments of memory. If Korea
emerges here adjacent to the cold war politics of left and
right, at the same time, it strikes me that the catastrophe of
war is completely embedded in the catastrophic scene of
our domestic.

Affliction

May 7, 1987. It was going to be Mother's Day in a few days. In the week before or so, I had made drawings for my mother and pasted them on construction paper. I was going to give them to my mother when she had her breakfast in bed— sunny-side up eggs with toast and orange juice. My older brother Mike always made the breakfast and we (collectively called "the kids") would eagerly help out. I couldn't wait. I shared a drawing with her. There are several Moms here and there in the house. She's cooking, she's reading with us, she's folding the laundry. I tell her that even though I am a difficult child, I know that she does everything for us, and I do not want her to fall off a cliff. When she was exasperated with us for one reason or another, our mother would always say, "And if I fell off a cliff, what would happen?"

It's raining. It's night. My siblings and I are in the car in the parking lot of the St. Vincent Hospital in Santa Fe, where my mother had undergone emergency brain surgery for a stroke. Joe, my father's friend, a short, balding man with glasses, is in the parking lot. My father is hugging him, sobbing. I had taken my drawing when we went to see our mother in the intensive care unit, but when I'm in the car, I realize that it has slipped out of my hand. I see it from the window, in a puddle, just a few steps from the car. But I just can't open the car door to pick it up.

While our mother was in the ICU, my twin brother, sister, and I spent our time sitting and sleeping in the pink and turquoise sofas of the waiting room and in a concrete outdoor patio area. I am reading *The Diary of Anne Frank*. I overhear our father say to our older brother Mike that he does not want "the kids to get scarred" by our mother's loss. Mom is moved from the ICU to another room. She is getting spasms in her legs; she is in severe pain. My sister calls the nurse, a fat woman with a short blond bob, white hospital pants and top. Keys jangling from a string around her neck. She angrily flexes and stretches Mom's legs, dropping each one onto the bed as she turns to the other. "You kids have to know that we have a lot of patients on this floor, so you can't expect me to run up to your mom if she has a problem, got it?" I'm too overwhelmed to speak and just hold Mom's hand. We say to Mom, "Wake up, Mom, wake up." The doctor wants to know if our mother responds to pain. He pinches her skin on the sternum. Her eyes widen and tear up. She's grabbing my sister's hands. The pinch was so brutal, it leaves a raised, knotted scar that she has until her death. I can feel a kernel of rage in me growing. As an adult and in the company of my closest friends, I start to see how that rage got routed into moralism. I want to recover that rage.

My father tells us not to cry at school. I don't remember crying. The other kids heard something happened at our house. The ambulance in front of the house—the neighbors notice; they talked. Mom is in the hospital, I tell them. Presbyterian church members give my siblings and me rides to the hospital in Santa Fe after school. They bring over casseroles. The church members call my mother "Joan." They tell us, "Your mom is a tough cookie." My chest tightens: how can they say this if they do not know her name?

There is a nurse named Joan. She works in the ICU and wears pink scrubs. She is thin and has sandy brown-blond hair. She is a comforting presence. After her shift, she takes my siblings and me to her house in Santa Fe. The adobe house is in the red-brown rolling hills dotted by tumbleweed and pine. We meet her son, who is smaller than us. The windows are open in the house. Thick, yellow pollen coats the heavy wood furniture. I run my finger through it in amazement. In the evening, my father picks us up from Joan's house.

My father moves our mother from the hospital in Santa Fe to St. Joseph Rehabilitation Center in Albuquerque. Every weekend, we drive two hours and stay at the Embassy Suites motel so we can visit her. (My father tells us much later that the only way he could afford all this, after being fired, was because our mother had saved for our college fund, which he used to cover the costs of care.) We meet the other patients in the ward. Victoria is a young woman who had a head injury from a car accident. Her long blond hair is tied up in a bun on top of her head, with wisps of hair framing her face. She slurs her words and has a distant look in her eyes, like many brain injury patients on the ward. But she is the ward's success story. The nurses tell us that Victoria rode a horse as part of her physical therapy. Jimmy has black hair and a salt-and-pepper beard. He always wears black T-shirts emblazoned with the names of heavy metal bands and black jeans. He is constantly chattering, repeating phrases over and over again, laughing at his own repetitions, and repeating his laugh as a repetition. But sometimes he needs to be restrained by the staff, and he screams and screams. My father befriends Jimmy and plays chess with him in his room. From my mother's room, I hear my father bantering with Jimmy. Why does he spend so much time with Jimmy and so little time with Mom? Paul is the father of two girls that are younger than my sister, twin brother, and me. Paul also had a stroke. Like our mother, he cannot speak or voluntarily move. He has dusty brown hair peppered with gray. His two girls playfully push him in the wheelchair, "Papa, now we're going down the hall. Papa, now we're going up the hall." Like our mother, he has not made sufficient progress in rehabilitation to be able to stay. My father speaks to his wife. Paul will go to a nursing home. I hear our father yelling at Dr. Nguyen, the neurologist.

Mom is home. The family room furniture is replaced by a hospital bed, wheelchair, and standing table. Dad tells Mike that they have to "talk," and Mike looks angry as he follows Dad into the living room. The doors are shut. In the kitchen, later, Dad is looking at Mom's "CAT scans." Mike is looking down at the kitchen floor. "Brain pressure." They, Los Alamos Hospital, St. Vincent Hospital—the waiting time before surgery, during surgery, afterward, it went terribly wrong, they are covering it up, the massive brain damage they caused. Dad is muttering on the phone to someone. He's on the phone a lot. "COBRA," "disability," "workman's comp." Alyse and I are learning how to change Mom's clothes, to turn her, to lift her up in the bed. The nurse grabs one side of the drawsheet, Alyse and I standing on the same side, take a corner each. I pull with as much strength as I can. So heavy. How did it happen that my sister and I do all of this now by ourselves? How slowly it dawned on us, from Santa Fe to Albuquerque rehab to our home, that Mom *might not* wake up.

But what does Mom know, what does she perceive? I am sitting with her in the family room. My twin brother and sister are at tennis practice. We rotate the responsibilities of taking care of Mom after school. Mom is in the wheelchair. She and I are looking out of the sliding glass doors to the backyard. Robins are hopping around the long grass underneath the rusting jungle gym that my siblings and I used to swing from. I do not know why a wave of grief hits me then, after years of taking care of Mom. I hug her and cry, pleading with her to please wake up. When my senses somewhat return to me, I find my mother has a tear running down her cheek. Do you know what has happened? Can you hear me? Do you understand what I am saying? Please wake up. We need you.

We receive packages of medicine from Korea. Our father says that they are from Auntie Young. The medicine is in a large red box that is separated into smaller cubbies. Each of the cubbies holds a ball of medicine, sealed in a packet. My twin brother Andy's chore is to give our mother medicine and give her regular feedings of Ensure, liquid nutrition, through a gastrointestinal tube. He drops the ball of medicine into a measuring cup of warm water and it slowly dissolves, releasing a pungent smell. When I visit Seoul thirty years later, my friend Professor Taewoo Kim takes me into the medicine market in Dongdaemun. I just tell him, "I know that smell."

My father tries to keep a rhythm to the household. He makes a big turkey with stuffing for Thanksgiving, with cranberry sauce and mashed potatoes. He makes bulgogi in the summer, and we grill it outside on the Weber, bringing our mother outside to enjoy the sun. Andy still cracks jokes and makes our father laugh. Dad says, "We still can laugh, can't we?" But the smallest of mistakes release explosions of fury. Household objects become landmines. The cap on the tube of toothpaste is left off. My father flies into a rage. Misplaced keys morphs into my siblings and me kneeling on the floor, heads bent down, while we are berated. Even as a very small child, I always had the impulsive need to clean up and arrange things; household chores give me an intense satisfaction. I folded my sister's clothes that she left in a heap next to the dresser in our bedroom and put them in neat little piles. At school, I cleaned the art supplies during recess when the other kids were playing outside. This impulse to clean and arrange intensified with my father's rages—I find myself scrubbing the bathroom at two in the morning as a high school student, reveling in the spotless ceiling in the shower and sparkling glass doors.

Dad is taking a toothpick from a brown ceramic holder on the kitchen counter. Dad says that Mom's favorite opera singer is Maria Callas, and Callas singing *Norma* is played over and over again in the house. I'm sitting at the dinner table, reading but not reading a book, hearing Dad clear his throat. He goes to the garage to smoke Kent cigarettes, slamming the door. I jump, my heart is pounding.

§

Our father says that my sister Alyse convinced him that our mother had to come back home, that she could not go to a nursing home. He says that Alyse was the conscience of our family, a pillar in this catastrophe. But what was it to bear that? My father had particular narratives of my sister, twin brother, and me—whether these narratives are life-giving or death-dealing, or both, and how so, keeps changing in our lives. Not only was my sister the conscience of our family, she was the most brilliant of all of the Han siblings. As a curse, it meant that she came to project such expectations of excellence for herself that anything short of winning a Nobel Prize would be a failure. My twin brother was a kind and gentle soul. But he did not excel enough in school. This meant that he would be put under terrible pressure to succeed in ways that simply did not conform with what made him happy.

However, I was the one who, my father said, should not have been born. In his daily banter, my father constantly cast me as selfish and competitive. My tendency to be a chatterbox repeatedly was cast as superficiality and attention-seeking. During his rages, though, the narrative was lethal. I was the child who murdered her mother, evil incarnate. In a blind rage the day after my mother fell ill, my father pointed to me, saying that my mother tripped over a music stand, causing her to have a massive stroke. I was practicing violin in my mother's bedroom and had left the music stand to the side of the door the night before my mother had her stroke. When my father found my mother, he found the music stand fallen down, next to her. As an "adult with a medical degree," I know that this story makes little sense in terms of disease etiology, yet as a child and even still now, the story has come to be deeply embedded in me as well as in the family. In an everyday spat with my siblings, this was the story that would shut me up, for which I had no response. And my siblings, in the rush to have the last word, would always deeply regret wounding me in this way when they lent their bodies to the voice of my father's rage.

My father hooked this story to my unexpected birth. The story went that our mother and father did not know that our mother was pregnant with twins. Andy was born first, and they were elated with the baby boy. The physicians expected the placenta to be born, but I came out next, and our mother cried. How could she handle having twins? Our father relates that he was happy with the twins, "the more the merrier," he had said. But after my mother's stroke, the "one who should not have existed" circling round my childhood took on a renewed intensity. I felt that the fact that I existed was somehow "against nature"—I was a monster. This feeling, however, carried with it a sense of victimhood hooked to a sense of extraordinary power—as if a child could single-handedly destroy the whole fabric of a world. One strangely becomes both victim and omnipotent god. Investing a child with such delusions of power and utter vulnerability makes her deeply fear herself but also think of herself as an epicenter. A strange empowerment, I became scrupulously careful around others, monster that I was.

As a child, perhaps one of the few respites from this narrative was my fascination and love for animals. Every Sunday evening, I watched *Nature* and *Wild, Wild World of Animals* on the PBS channel. I spent hours looking at the *Encyclopedia Britannica*'s entry on dogs. I knew each breed by heart and still do. I was the one who took care of our dogs and spent the most time with them. Our first dog was Pepper, a small gray, black, and brown long-haired terrier mutt, who has a terrible habit of peeing on the carpet. My siblings and I come back from church one day to discover that my father had adopted her, much to my mother's chagrin. Pepper is fourteen years old when she starts becoming exhausted while walking. It's the middle of the night, and I'm with her in my bedroom while she is gasping for breath. I somewhat futilely attempt to give her mouth-to-nose resuscitation, which I learned from a television show on veterinary medicine. After her last breath, I carry Pepper out to the family room, where our mother is lying in her hospital bed. My father is awake. I tell him Pepper died. She feels so heavy in my arms. I can only remember him acting in a flurry, grabbing Pepper from me. "Don't hold it!" he yells, with a fear-tinged voice. He doesn't call her Pepper. It's as if he feels a deep revulsion at seeing me, a child or his daughter, hold a dead animal, as if it hits up against a limit. Was I sometimes just a child to my father, or just his daughter—a member of the family—and not the monster that I thought I was? How strange it is that holding a dead animal can reveal a father's love or, at the very least, an acknowledgment that his daughter was human.

§

The reverberations of my mother's illness, her death, and the lethality that grew in me have made their appearance in different ways over the years. I find it difficult to say that there is any single kernel of "trauma" that progressively reveals itself. Instead, these reverberations crisscross the flux of my life. In my first years of graduate school, I find that the incredible sense of power and utter vulnerability I felt as a child had morphed into a desperate sense of desolation. First, I stay in my room in a shared apartment, surrounded by my books, reading with a frantic feeling. It pains me today to see those

dark, deep self-absorbed pencil marks underscoring passages
in those books, unable to read the text as a text written by
another. Later, it is the inverse—I am a social butterfly, engaging in the usual graduate student squabbles, hanging out
in bars, engaging in fleeting sexual trysts. But, I can't keep
any of the pettiness at the surface, and each squabble, un-
toward remark, fling gone bad drives me into an anger that
further hollows me out. I seek exits with mentors: postdoctoral fellows, my faculty committee members. They are outside "the fray"; they are lifelines. One of my committee
members asks me if I have "suicidal ideation." I deny it but
know that something is terribly wrong. Circling round the
impulse to take my life, I find myself in a period of intense
self-examination as a patient of the Victims of Violence Unit
at the Cambridge Hospital. I am seen regularly for over a year
by a Brazilian psychoanalyst who challenges me to examine
what that strange satisfaction is in the tone of my voice when
I tell him that my father made me into a destroyer of worlds.
But it may be fieldwork, where I meet a "twin soul" who
shares with me the struggles over violence and care in her
own family, that allows me to see *again* how utterly difficult
it is to be present to another being.

  After I met my husband, Maarten, other lethal dimen-
sions of our mother's illness revealed themselves. When we
moved to Baltimore as a young couple, well-meaning friends
and colleagues would ask me when (not if) we would have a
child. For the most part, I resorted to our fears surrounding
job security, my own and Maarten's, to explain why we were
not having children. The experience of tenure track was indeed serious. Our family receives health benefits through my
employment. Neither of us come from families that are fi-
nancially able to help us if I lost my job. But it was also that
the thought of having a child infuriated me. Each time a colleague or friend suggested I should have children or asked

me when I would, I could feel myself seething: a pot of mol-
ten iron bubbling over that would burn and lay waste to the
entire world. The sheer thought of having a child felt like a
threat to my existence, and I would do anything to defend
the existence that I had.

Some years ago, I discovered when speaking to my sister
that she too shared this linking of reproduction and lethality. Our brothers, however, had children earlier and seemed
immune to these feelings. Having borne the brunt of daily
care of our mother as children, perhaps we learned that there
is a lethality to full-blown care, a care that is also the very
physicality of bearing and caring for children. This lethality
is not adequately described in terms of a moralistic notion
of "self-sacrifice" and it gets suppressed in the accounts of
care as life-sustaining or as attentiveness. It's that the very
labors of care can nourish the most threatening, most dark
aspects of ourselves: that I could spill over, burn and lay waste
to an entire world.

I do not know how this lethality quieted down in me. A
friend and colleague once suggested to me that it was because
I had embedded myself in genealogy—that is, reconnected
with relatives in Korea and undertaken the writing of this
book—that made it possible for Ella to be born. I am unsure
of such explanations. There is so much more that others do
not know and so much more that I do not know of myself. I
think it is a miracle that I met Maarten and that we have a
beautiful daughter Ella.

Fragments

When I try to recall the contexts in which my father spoke
of his mother, of his childhood, of war, I find that I cannot
myself recall how I know these fragments, when they were
told, and under what circumstances. It is as if the context of

telling is, for the most part, not available to me, but the affects around the telling are still very much alive. I have come
to wonder if the dispersed qualities of storytelling were related to both my father's telling as well as my ability to listen. For indeed, there were times that I simply could not
listen to my father's stories, or times when I was listening,
simply because these were the times when his words seemed
so alive.

§

My father says: "My mother was so beautiful. She had blond
hair and blue eyes, the beauty of the village. She had such
resentment, I remember her crying, 'Sook-Jong, Sook-Jong'
[my Dad's name]. I never saw my father's face, because I always looked down." (My father gestures, his head bowing
down to the floor. I am watching my father.) I imagine my
grandmother, Dad's mother, her blond hair and blue eyes,
in a hanbok, a faded pink top and blue skirt. I imagine her
in a small thatched hut crying by herself and see my Dad as
a child watching her cry. Dad's father is a "businessman." My
imagination of the businessman (my grandfather) is not his
face but (Dad's, and my) seeing the bottom half of dark navy
pants and shiny black leather shoes, accompanied by a feeling of fear and dread. Dad's mom was sold by her parents to
this man so her brothers could have an education. Dad tells
us that his mom was so bitter that she never had a chance to
go to school. Dad said: "I picked berries with my sister, whole
buckets of berries. We would run into the river with nets and
catch bags and bags of these small fish. We got into the water
and got soaked, and my brother and I walked home. I knew
we were going to get in trouble." (He makes the gesture to
show how tiny the fish were.) I imagine green bushes dotted
by blackberries, buckets and buckets of blackberries, eating
them while walking back, buckets on our backs, over hills
and up mountain paths. Walking down to a bubbling stream,

behind my brother, seeing so many swirls of little fish in the
eddies of the stream, scooping them up with nets, falling into
the stream, laughing. Walking home and shivering from the
cold, scolded by Uncle. He makes us stand with books over
our heads for hours. "Uncle was such a good man," Dad says.
The planes are dropping bombs. Dad says they were running
to the train station. He says: "But I had my pet bunny at
home. What would happen to the bunny? I was crying. My
mom says that I can run home and hammer planks of wood
over the bunny's cage. Meet us at the train station. I come
back to the train station and get on the train, but I don't see
my mother. The trains are moving and I hear my mother
screaming, 'Sook-Jong, Sook-Jong!' I got on the wrong train,
going the wrong direction. She is waving her arms out of the
train. We pass each other, going different directions. This is
the last time I saw my mother."

§

"Oh, it was tough," Dad tells us. "We were on a boat, and
ate one rice ball a day. Did you know that underneath the
bark of trees there is a layer of pulp that you can eat? That's
why I have so many problems with my teeth now."

§

Dad is washing the dishes, and it just so happens that a spoon
is seesawing back and forth under the running water. The
spoon is delicately balanced on the handle of a dirty pot. Dad
says to me, "Look at that!" He explains how this seesawing
motion works in relation to the viscosity of water. "I learned
physics this way," Dad says. "I didn't go to school, I learned
it from watching, observing. Kids lived in cardboard boxes
on the street. We took Coca-Cola cans and split them, in
two—it was amazing—chaaaa—right down the middle of the
can, and we lay them on top of each other to make a roof. In
the wintertime, it is so cold, but I needed to study. I had the
ink bottle and tied a string around and hung it around my

neck under my clothes. Then, I can keep writing and the ink doesn't freeze."

Five Red Roses

My father calls my sister. My sister calls me. Mom died. I run to Alyse's dorm room. Andy is sitting in a chair. Alyse is hugging him. Our mother has died as we were taking the flight back to New Jersey to return to Princeton for winter intersession, to study for our final exams. Before we left home, our father and older brother fought bitterly. They were yelling in the kitchen at each other. My brother leaves early before we celebrate the holidays together. Mom, did you know? Are you saying that it was your time? Were you trying to protect us, waiting until we left, so we wouldn't see you die?

Our father refuses to let us come back for her funeral, insisting that we need to study. We call our older brother, Mike. He is in New Jersey with his girlfriend, Virginia. He takes us to the airport. Screaming at the man at the ticketing counter, he says, "You are telling me that you will not help these kids go to their mother's funeral. Their mother just died!" Virginia says, "It's okay, Mike. It's okay." She takes out her credit card and pays for all of our tickets. We make it to Albuquerque. Reverend Parker and his wife, Joanne, have moved there and we spend the night in their home. Our father arrives in the morning. We drive back to Los Alamos, to the funeral home. I'm in the car, looking out the back window. My father is walking across the parking lot with my older brother. Suddenly, he slips on the ice. Mike grabs hold of him. My father appears so very frail.

No one is invited to the funeral, except for the other Hahn family, who were our neighbors for several years. One of the few Korean families in town, my mother had become friends with Mrs. Hahn and, up until my mother's illness, we spent our days in each other's houses. Mr. Hahn and one of their sons, Matthew, help carry my mother's coffin with my twin brother and older brother. Mrs. Hahn is quietly weeping. There are no floral arrangements. My sister and older brother cannot bear burying our mother without a single flower. They buy five red roses, which we throw onto the coffin as it is lowered into the ground. This is the last time our older brother sees our father.

Dreams

A few years ago, my sister set up our father with an iPad, so he could speak to us on video chat. I call him while I am in Seoul. Dad says to me he had a strange dream and that he was telling that dream to Alyse just earlier today. "What was the dream?" I ask. He recounts, "I was just falling asleep, and I hear someone say into my ear that I could eat something sweet." He seems to change the topic, "I was looking at Mom's picture for a long time today." I am seeing the picture of Mom that Dad has kept next to the rocking chair in the living room since Mom passed away. A black-and-white picture when she was maybe in her early twenties, in a white blouse and a wavy bob haircut. "I was thinking how did we get to this point, how did all of this happen?" He goes on, "You know I have a younger sister." "Yes." "A younger sister four years younger than the older sister you met." (Was this the sister he picked berries with? Dad never once says directly that she is in the North—it does not need to be said.) "Oh, she was your older sister too?" I ask. "Yes, she was such a gentle and kind soul. And I was wondering why Mom had us dispersed, all the kids dispersed to other relatives. Why didn't she just keep us all together?" I realize Dad is talking not about our Mom but about his Mom, our grandmother.

"Then, I got it. It was such a crisis during those times. We were in crisis. You know there wasn't any food, no rice. Mom couldn't feed all of us. So she had to disperse us to different relatives. When the war started, we thought it would last a month, then it would be over, then it didn't stop, all of us refugees, it lasted forever . . . Then, I go to sleep and I have this sweet dream," Dad laughs.

Our mother is buried in Guaje Pines Cemetery in Los Alamos. Although we held her funeral over twenty years ago, she does not have a tombstone. My father has said that he is still trying to find the right words to put on the grave. My siblings and I wait; we know that our father may not find these words, and we will and must be the ones to find them. When I visit my father, he takes me and my husband to the cemetery to see her grave. He remembers where she is buried and has arranged for a plot for them to be buried next to each other when he dies. I remark to my father that the cemetery seems smaller than I remember. My father says, "Yes, not many people get buried here. They go back to their homes. It's for those of us who don't have a home."

I've often recounted to others that my mother and father were displaced from "the North." It is perhaps a way to evade the more fundamental displacement of a Korean language shattered by war and by affliction. Our family lived a displacement from homemaking in life, a catastrophe at the level of the domestic in the loss of my father's wife and our mother. We are all, in our different ways, trying to simply "get home." I responded to my father's words with a banal yet totally earnest statement, "But Dad, you have a home with your kids, don't you?" He didn't reply.

My mother has not come to me in dreams for many years. The last dream with her was some years ago, after I moved to Baltimore with Maarten. She was in the front seat of her green VW bug, and I was in the back seat. I am a small child.

There is a beautiful red Irish setter dog in the passenger seat of the car. My mother is wearing a fur coat, its brown and white fluffy trim covering her neck. Her hands are in brown leather fur-trimmed gloves, and I see the shine of pearl earrings on her ears. Her hair is black and wavy. She is wearing lipstick. Mom is awake! I'm too afraid to exclaim to her that she is awake. But she says to me, "Clara, I woke up. I'm here." She is incredibly beautiful. She backs the car out of the driveway of our house in New Mexico, and suddenly we are in grassy green hills. The car door is open. In a tan dress with a sparkling brooch, my mother is standing in the grass, fur coat now slung around her shoulders. Her hand is shading her eyes from the sun. She's watching me run gleefully up and down the hillsides. The Irish setter is running circles around us. I am fighting to stay asleep. When I wake, the feeling of Mom having woken up, having returned as the princess, is so strong that I lie in bed for a while within that reality. As the morning sounds come from the street, a wave of sadness washes over me.

Interlude 1
Affliction and War in the Domestic

To whom do these memories belong? While we often think of memory in terms of the individual, here what emerges is the family as the subject of memory—much like illness might be understood not as simply located within a body but rather as involving a whole host of relationships, shifting affects, and encounters to which that body may give expression (Das 2015a). Here, we might mark a clear contrast between family pictured as one among several nested units (individual, family, nation) and family as the scene of intimate relations, permeated by forces such as war, migration, discrimination, and unemployment. Whereas seeing the family as a socio-logical unit tends to reproduce dominant narratives of the family as a "mini-nation," the family as a scene of intimate relations brings to the fore the contests over the real. Like illness experience, there is no one single coherent story in these memories, no single narrative that organizes experi-ence, and thus nothing to "transmit." Rather, there are sto-ries that are revived, recast in their retelling, their tone and intensity shifting in the flux of our lives.

In the scenes above, war is dispersed into illness that devastated domestic life and appears in the dark threats that grow out of the very love and care that sustain that life. Affliction here seems to be the scene for my childhood memories not only because it marked my childhood life but also because of what affliction is and can do to domestic life and to oneself. As Myra Bluebond-Langner's pathbreaking study in a children's cancer ward reveals, children can be starkly aware of their own dying, revealing that knowledge of affliction and death do not necessarily align with the assumed boundaries that separate the category of children from that of adults (Bluebond-Langner 1978). When we move from the scene of the clinic to the scene of the domestic, however, we see perhaps more acutely that children learn affliction in ways that are not cordoned off from other aspects of life; learning affliction is part and parcel of the child's piecing together of a world. Yet, affliction can bring the child into darker regions of this world and deform categories of understanding that are not yet stable. Perhaps these darker recesses of everyday life, made available through affliction, is where, as a child, I also felt the impress of war on myself.

In the scene of affliction, catastrophes reverberate in foreboding landscapes of childhood, in the lethality of care, and in the devastating betrayals that appear in the most quotidian of gestures. War, illness and dying, betrayals in the family are interwoven with each other. This quality of crisscrossing stories and impressions, of vastly different scales, may relate to the plain and simple fact of childhood itself. Children do not have stable categories like adults do. They are learning these categories. They are piecing impressions, gestures, things, and words together bit by bit. In my memories of this piecing together, I strangely discover that the child's voice seems to usher forth life as a whole and perhaps brings me closer to staking a claim in this life as my own.

In an extremely perceptive essay, Richard Rechtman makes the distinction between the subjectivization of experience and subjective experience. Subjectivization of experience can be understood as a "construction" or "performance" that comes in the form of a chronological narrative that is, in a sense, "ethnographically fictional." In discussing testimony, Rechtman writes:

> One can learn from these writings about incredible horrors that one could not have imagined before. Then one can imagine what the terrible looks like under those dramatic circumstances. But this is much more a tale or a fiction that helps those who were not there to understand, from their perspective, standing outside of those events, what could have happened to them. It gives a possible identification with victims because, behind this indescribable horror, everything looks the same as what people experience under "usual" conditions. . . . Those stories give us a tale, or a narrative, that borrows its parameters from usual types of experience, but it is based on a denial, at the same time, of all other parameters that in fact determine the sense of the everyday of these extreme situations. All those testimonies are then historically true, but ethnographically fictional. (Rechtman 2017, 138)

The "fictional" is the attempt to create an understandable narration retrospectively to outsiders by highlighting traumatic events as they are tied to major events.[1] But, extreme violence in the everyday is a nonevent, absorbed into the ordinary. It is only after the fact that these circumstances become "traumatic events" rendered in narrative form. Fragments of experience, however, may not fit this chronological narrative. They cannot simply be absorbed—or renarrativized—into the categories of psychiatry, trauma theory, or local idioms of distress. Such fragments Rechtman calls "echoes of suffering."

Rechtman makes the distinction between everyday life in extreme violence and the "usual conditions" of everyday life, which are assumed to have stable separations of reality and delusion. But we can also consider the different perspectives within everyday life in contexts that are not currently lived under extreme violence. From the perspective of the child, boundaries between reality, fantasy, and dream are permeable, such that the "reality frontiers" or the "boundaries of time" that testimony presumes are simply not available to the child. To put it another way, the child does not have the vocabulary at hand to articulate a narration that would establish a historical perspective. These vocabularies are learned, part of what it means to participate in a form of life, and cannot be assumed in advance. And for the parents who might invite the child into a future in language, they are shadowed by powerful and enduring skepticism about one's belonging. If one's footing in the world is always somehow unsure, in such cases, the routes through which one might have found their way into language bear the marks of that violence. If Rechtman acutely shows how testimony avoids the everyday of extreme violence, his analysis also reveals how testimony avoids the child and the picture of the everyday that her perspective can offer.

In affliction, we can hear the echoes of suffering from catastrophic violence. These echoes are not marked out from everyday life. They resound in the child's making sense of the world, infusing her learning kinship, affliction, and death. In this way, the child inherits familial memories of violence in the inhabitation of everyday life. How the child absorbs these memories and what voice she finds in them, then, is an open question, and one to which this writing is a response.

PART II

A Future in Kinship, a Future in Language

In January of 2015, I went to Seoul to take a three-week Korean course at Seoul National University. Through a set of contingencies, my sister had located and been in intermittent touch with one of my mother's younger sisters who lives in Seoul. A social worker who worked with my sister at San Francisco General Hospital is from Korea. She graduated from Ewha Womans University, where our aunt had also graduated. The social worker contacted the university's alumni association network. It turned out that the secretaries knew our aunt well. She had been the treasurer and the secretary of the association. They contacted our aunt. Shortly before I left for Seoul, my sister forwarded our aunt's email address to me, and I wrote to tell her. Here is an excerpt from a journal I kept when I first went to Seoul in January of 2015:

> Maarten and I are in Auntie Young and her husband's apartment, where Auntie Young had prepared

a family dinner, welcoming me into the family. After dinner. Auntie Young takes out a photo album. "I have pictures of you from when I visited." Green and blue with a butterfly and white lettering in English on the cover. The first pictures are of Mike [my older brother] when he was a baby. These are the same pictures that I have seen growing up. That we have in our houses. The picture of Dad holding Mike when he was a baby—I have that picture framed and in my bedroom in Baltimore. The picture of Mike smiling, Mike has that picture enlarged and framed in his house in Seattle. "See. When you were born. [Our birthdates.]" Written on the first page. Photos of us as small children, and growing up. Nearly every year of our lives. Mom sent the pictures of us, family pictures, to Auntie Young. The pictures stopped at the time when Mom got sick.

Auntie Young tells me that she had come to the US for an international pharmaceutical conference in Montreal. She took a short trip to New Mexico to visit Mom and Portland Oregon to visit Auntie Myung.

1987—This is the year that Auntie Young visited us in New Mexico. She has pictures of us from her visit. But this is the same year that Mom got ill. The same year of her stroke . . . I was 11 years old. But, why then did I remember and write to Auntie Young that she visited when I was only 5 years old? Why do I remember barely being able to see over a handrail, being a very small child at the time of her visit? Does [it] have something to do with the experience of adult role, of adult knowledge, after my mother's illness?

Auntie Young (whom I now call *Imo*) was waiting for me at Incheon International Airport. As we pass through passport control, Maarten asks me, "How will you know who Auntie Young is?" I had not considered the possibility that I would not be able to recognize her. As we come out to the arrivals hall, however, Maarten yells, "Clara, there she is, there she is!" Maarten had seen a woman, holding a sign with "Welcome Clara" in English. My eyes hurriedly scan the hall, and before I see the sign, I see my mother. That is, standing just over there is a woman who looks so much like my mother. Suddenly the hall is blanketed with shadows; my being as a whole is jarred. My aunt greets me, and I begin to cry; I can't help myself. She asks me in Korean, "Why are you crying? Don't cry." Her husband speaks to me in English, saying that they did not know how they were going to find me in the rush of people coming into the arrival hall. So they made this welcome sign. But my aunt saw me and saw her sister. She knew me before having met me, through her sister.

She and her husband take us to the hotel where we will spend the first two nights. As we get out of the car, she looks around the hotel lobby, perhaps checking it out to see if it is adequate. I recognize that look of concern. The tightness of the jaw, the slightly furrowed brow. Again, I see my mother. It's as if she is overlaid onto my aunt. An image comes to me—in her tan London Fog jacket, with jeans on. Wavy, short hair with glasses. We're in the parking lot of the Smith's supermarket in White Rock, New Mexico. Mom lets me, my sister, and twin brother out of the car, and we are bolting toward the supermarket entrance. She tries to chase after us but trips over a parking lot bump and twists her ankle, falling. She says, "Ccchhh," rubbing her ankle. We run back. "Let's start over," she says, getting up and dusting off, going back to the car, and walking back to the store again. She doesn't chide us. But I feel my face getting hot and red with shame for making her fall, for the unruly pack of kids that we are (or were).

Two days later, Maarten and I have moved into a small studio apartment in the Gangnam neighborhood, and I begin intensive Korean classes at Seoul National University. The afternoon I return from classes, the concierge of the building ushers me over to a large box that has my name on it in English. My aunt had left the box during the day. It was filled with rice and kimchi. She comes to visit again and again with her husband. Sometimes in the afternoons when we are not in, she leaves a box of kimchi and rice; sometimes in the evening, she comes to see how we are doing. I struggle to speak to her in my limited Korean; her husband, who is fluent in English, translates between us. By the end of the three weeks, I come to realize that I am calling her Imo. She is our aunt, the sister of our mother. The shadows start to dissipate. I might put it this way: As she emerges to me as Imo, I begin to see the shadows that overcame my senses. That, upon meeting her in the airport, I did not really "meet" her but rather was re-encountering my mother's death. It was through the back and forth with Imo, her persistence in simply being and becoming our aunt, that our mother reappeared again—that is, her life—through the connection that aunt and niece are making with each other.

I return to Seoul for the summer of 2015 for three months of intensive language training in Korean at Seoul National University. Now I am staying in an apartment on campus, and again, Imo comes to help set up the apartment, but now with her oldest daughter, Kyung Mi. With boxes of rice, kimchi, *miyŏkkuk*, sliced watermelon, and *boricha*. They come with bedding and kitchen equipment, utensils, and dishware. The classes start again. Students are required to take a placement test at the beginning of the course. I take the written test and am interviewed in Korean by a teaching faculty. He decides that while I am "slightly under" intermediate Korean level, because I am a professor, I "should be challenged." I am thrown into a level for which I am totally unprepared. I am studying like mad—eyes bloodshot, undersleeping— like a college student worried about passing a final exam. In a panic, I write a text to Kyung Mi, asking her to tutor me. She agrees, and we begin to meet once a week in my small apartment, sharing lunch, and chatting in Korean about the news, about schooling and the anxiety around the national exam, the relationships of daughters-in-law and mothers-in-law, the politics of real estate in Seoul, about postpartum depression.

I meet Imo for lunches and dinners, and as my ability in Korean improves, we are able to meet by ourselves, without her husband and the difficult position he was put in as "translator." On a visit to the contemporary art museum together, Imo asks me why we did not learn Korean at home. I sense that she knows something and is seeking to confirm her suspicions. I tell her that our father was quite opposed to our learning Korean. Imo is quiet, then responds, "Your mother was a magnificent person." It suddenly strikes me: what kind of labor of love was entailed in not speaking Korean to us but to speak in a tongue (English) that was not fully mastered, allowing one to become vulnerable in certain ways to one's children, and to speak in a tongue in which one had such difficulty in conveying the affects one had for one's children. What was it for my mother to have her language cut off from her children by her husband, who felt that we should have no relation to Korea, who would have us inherit this betrayal, and who saw us as his revenge on the world, in a world that was at war with itself?

It struck me that day as I was talking to my aunt, the deep cuts that my father had put into my mother's relationships with her sisters when, for instance, my father had harshly

scolded my mother's older sister—who was visiting from Portland, Oregon, when we were small children—for teaching
us Korean words, which we eagerly sopped up. Auntie Myung
was tall and slender; she wore a nightgown and robe, her hair
in a towel, even though it was the middle of the day. With
curiosity, my sister and I watched her cut up potatoes and eat
them raw. She was in my older brother's room, with my sister
and twin brother. I'm hovering around the living room, about
to join them. I heard her speaking in Korean to them, repeating words—puppy "강아지." But then the sound of the door
opening brusquely, angry bursts from my father to Auntie
Myung in Korean, barking. The door slams. The repetition
stops. The room is silent.

§

My sister Alyse is taking a fiction writing seminar. She sends
me a story she wrote, a story ignited by a memory of Auntie
Myung. Her story is entitled "Raw Potatoes" and begins with
a description of a fictionalized character—our Auntie
Myung—in the backyard of our house, eating a raw potato
like an apple. In the story, the raw potato figures as both poison and medicine, that which keeps the fictional character
alive: the poison allows her to forget her past life, while at
the same time allowing her to live a new life in the United
States. Yet, that very poison allows her to visit her younger
sister (our mother) who lives in New Mexico. So, in some
sense, a region of her past/future is still alive to her, that of
her kinship relations. When I received the story, I called my
sister. How uncanny that we both had this memory-image
available to us in our writing. She does not recall our father
chastising Auntie Myung. What she does remember is a feeling that the trip was not a happy one.

At the end of the summer of 2015, my sister visits me in
Seoul, where she meets our Imo and our mother's second
youngest sister, Auntie Kyung (Changwon Imo), who lives in

Changwon, a city just next to the second largest city in Korea, Busan. She meets our paternal and maternal cousins and our father's older sister, our Komo. My sister had learned some basic Korean but needed me to be with her as a translator of sorts. She asks Imo about her work as a pharmacist. She wants to hear stories of our mother as a child. It is not easy to find Korean words for my sister's English words, to find the right tone for my sister's tone.

We are walking in the hot sun in the Hongdae neighborhood with Imo. We're getting worried that it is getting too hot for Imo to be outside. She looks tired, and there is sweat on her brow, even as she is shaded by a parasol. We duck into a small restaurant for lunch, where we are served kimchi *jjigae*. Imo's talk circumambulates around our mother's illness. She knew that our mother had been ill but did not know what the circumstances were and how, as a family, we had lived it. I try to describe the situation in our home, the chaos, the frictions. I relate this in Korean, turning to my sister to relate to her what I am saying in English. Imo eats quietly. My sister looks at me, as if to tell me not to reveal everything, that would be too wounding. Why make such memories of our mother for our aunt? Why not just allow our mother to live between us, among us, in the fact that we can speak to each other, eat together, today and hopefully tomorrow?

I return to Seoul again in June of 2016 for another intensive language course. I am twenty-six weeks pregnant with Ella, and the talk of the new baby pervades all of my conversations. I've decided that I will stay until thirty-two weeks and hope that the airline does not bar me from boarding a return flight back at that late stage. This time, I stay in the neighborhood where Imo and Kyung Mi live. In case anything happens, I am close to kin. Imo's younger daughter, Su Young, is a professor of obstetric medicine and practices at Samsung Hospital. She is concerned that I will not have a prenatal checkup during this entire time. She gives me an exam and does a 3D ultrasound on my belly—the first that I have ever had. She looks at the solid organs, the ventricles, the gut, and gauges the health of the placenta. It all looks fine, and I assume the exam will end. But she instructs the medicine fellow to try to get a picture of Ella's face, so we can see her face together. Ella's face is buried in her hands. She asks me to roll on one side. Now, roll to the other side. Ella seems to be sleeping; Su Young asks if she can wake her up by putting a small vibrating device onto my belly. I uneasily agree. Ella jumps, her hands come off her face. The medicine fellow quickly snaps the photo, and everyone coos to say how "cute" Ella is. It is the first time I see her face. I take the ultrasound picture and keep it on my desk until she is born.

§

When I began traveling to Seoul, my father asked me to find his sister, Ok Hie Han, and to locate his niece and nephew, daughter and son of his older brother with whom he had made the arduous journey by boat from Hungnam port in the North to Busan in the South when the United States army fled South during the Korean War, carpet-bombing as they fled. My father recounts how bombs dropped from the sky, he played with the unexploded bombs on fields, those whirring fans. He also recounts, though, his mother's worn feet, she can't walk anymore up the mountain path, the soldiers' (unsure of what side they are on) faces demoralized, she tells my father and his older brother to keep walking, leave her there. My father's brother and my father reached Busan and then finally ended up in their sister's house in Seoul, where they worked in her sister's husband's sweatshop. As my uncle's daughter (Sung Sook) related to me, he ended up drinking all day, crying for his mother whom they left. I learn from my cousins that their father too was "scary." I learn from Sung

Sook that we have an uncle and aunt still in the North. We are not sure if they are still alive. Our aunt, my father's older sister, was approached by the Red Cross in the 1980s to see if she would like to try to locate her younger siblings, but she decided against it. She couldn't bear to know what had happened to them.

I would only know this after meeting Sung Sook and after having walked the streets of the Hongdae neighborhood, looking for a house belonging to Ok Hie Han. Before my first visit to Seoul, my father emailed me his sister's house address. He tells me that he only has the street address, no phone number or email. But Seoul addresses had changed, so houses either had two addresses or only the new one. This made finding my father's sister's house quite difficult. My Korean teacher at the time puts me in touch with a friend, who accompanies me through the side streets of the Hongdae neighborhood, and we eventually find the house, a white house with two stories, set behind a black iron fence. The friend knocks on the first-floor door, but the woman who answers says that she had never heard of an Ok Hie Han. The friend goes upstairs and knocks, but no answer. She leaves a note at the door. Although I was carrying a gift in my hands for my father's sister—just learning to say "our aunt"—I know that she might not be alive. She would be ninety years old. The friend has tears in her eyes. I am a bit lost in my own thoughts—rehearsing ways to tell my father that I have not been able to find her. As I return from Seoul, however, I receive an email from my father's sister's youngest daughter. My father had had her email address this whole time.

My father's sister's youngest daughter, Chung Ran, meets me when I return in the summer of 2015. She drives a luxury car. She speaks English fluently. Over lunch, she asks me again and again about my visit to her mother's house, scoffing when I say that the woman who lived on the first floor had never heard of Ok Hie Han. "She must not have wanted to tell a stranger." She asks me, "But no one answered the door?" I repeat that no one was there. She tells me that her older brother and sister are now occupying the house. She intimates that the siblings took advantage of their mother, pushed her out of her own home and forced her into a nursing home. Her talk ushers me into a set of tortuous relationships among the siblings. I sense uneasily that she wants me to know her version of the story, not so much for myself but to relay to my father, who, along with our aunt, is the last living member (as far as we know) of our parents' generation. She puts me in touch with our cousins, my father's older brother's daughter and son, saying that she would like to have a lunch together.

My father yearned to hear of what happened to his brother's children, if they were alive. He says to me that when he left Korea, Sung Sook was just one year old. She had been struck with polio as a baby and had lost the use of her legs. The son, Yong Chul, was born a few years later. I am writing to my father over email, sending short messages that I have gotten in touch with the cousins and will write back after I meet Sung Sook and Yong Chul. But before I meet them, he writes an email to me with the heading, "That was too much!" "Hope you survived the ordeal," he writes, "You could have just passed my message. In any case, I appreciate your time. . . . It is very tragic for my brother to endure such a heartbreaking pain. Just to let them know that we do care about them. How was Yong Chul? Thanks, Dad."

Sung Sook calls me on my cell phone. My ability to speak in Korean is rudimentary and even worse on the phone. I understand that she wants to meet, that she is picking me up early, and that I should be ready to go somewhere outside of Seoul. She picks me up with her husband. In the car, she shows me pictures of my father in Seoul in 1959 and 1960, pictures of his graduation from Seoul National University, pictures of their father and mother, my uncle and aunt. We drive to the countryside where Sung Sook and her husband have grown oleaster fruit on a small parcel of land. Picking fruits all day, taking pictures, talking—there's the strangest feeling of easy familiarity, we note this to each other. Sung Sook is unable to move her legs but gets around with crutches by leaning on one of her legs and moving her arms. Her husband, too, lives with disability. As a child, he was playing under a train, when the train moved and amputated his leg. He too moves with crutches.

Sung Sook seems sensitive to disability. Seoul is not an easy place for such a condition. I notice that people seem to ignore her or to move away from her in the street. It is as if her condition reminds people of the recent past. We go to a restaurant together, where there is floor seating, and she scoots on her bottom from where we leave our shoes to our table. The owner says nothing but looks at her. Sung Sook, says proudly, to the owner, "This is my cousin. She's from the United States and is a professor at Johns Hopkins University." The man nods. I nod back and smile. She goes on to say that I am visiting Seoul for the first time and that I am learning Korean because I want to work here. The man nods, but in the midst of the description, his eyes flit back and forth to the television in the corner.

A few weeks into the summer, Sung Sook invites me to her husband's seventieth birthday party where I meet her two utterly beautiful children in their mid-to-late twenties and early thirties. To have secured a life amid and through the stigma cast on disability is a remarkable achievement. They are exquisitely yet nonchalantly aware of their mother's and father's conditions, pulling out chairs for them to sit in, bringing them tea, getting food for them from the buffet. The daughter studied fashion design and is engaged to a *manhwa* artist. Her aunts and uncles call her "Miss Korea" in English—she really is absolutely stunning in her beauty. The son works at Samsung, is married, and has a son, a small toddler. Sung Sook's daughter takes an immediate liking to me, as I recount my trials and tribulations of Korean classes. She addresses me, "Imo [aunt], why don't you speak *ban-mal* to me?" Ban-mal is the shortened, informal form of address that elders would speak to the young or friends may speak to each other. I had been speaking to her in the polite form, which, in our position as kin, was incredibly awkward for her. I hadn't spoken in ban-mal before, in any situation, outside of a role play in the classroom. And I find myself stumbling between ban-mal and the polite form, marked by my niece's chuckles. I write my father a long email and send pictures. He writes back: "Incredible!" I talk to my father on Skype from Seoul, describing Sung Sook's children, her husband, and our conversations. My father says that he is relieved that Sung Sook found love. "Her father did not support her in getting married. Because of her condition, he never thought that anyone would want to marry her."

Sung Sook works in a currency exchange in Myeong Dong, a small white kiosk, in which she can sit on a pillow and attend to clients without revealing her disability. I visit her in the kiosk, spending days with her while she counts money to clients coming with dollars and euros. I related to her that I have met with our cousin Chung Ran and mention that it seems that there are frictions between the siblings. She gives me advice: "You say, yes, yes, and nothing more," and then throws in a bit of advice about how we respect our elders, "Just as you say 'yes' to your father, and bow, always showing respect." She relates to me how she would hide under the covers, shuddering, during her father's drunken tirades. She asks me about my meeting with our imo, and I relate to her how Imo brought rice and kimchi to my apartment and how affectionate she is. "Your imo comes from the Eastern side of the North. They are much warmer, effusive people. Our fathers and my mother come from the Western side. They are more strict and scary." The general talk of "scary" parents hints at specific darker textures to which I do not have access, nor does Sung Sook broach to me.

My father wants to be in direct contact with Sung Sook through email. Sung Sook has never set up an email address for herself. But, with the help of her son, she creates a Gmail account. She writes my father. My father forwards me the email. Why did the email come from a woman named Young Jin? Sung Sook ends the email to my father with the name "Sung Sook," but the email address itself is "Young Jin Han." My father is perturbed. He asks me if Sung Sook has changed her name. I quickly dismiss the possibility. But then, I realize that her Kakao ID (text ID for the chat app in Korea) is also Young Jin. Why would she have done this? My father writes repeated emails to me, "You tell Sung Sook that we do not change our names. You tell her to change her name back. We don't break the name." Sung Sook's name ties her genealogically and laterally to her generation through the practice of generational names called *dol lim ja*. By changing her name, Sung Sook breaks herself out of these kinship relations. This is what my father refers to as "breaking the name." Yet, in her relationship with me, my sister, and my father, she refers to herself as Sung Sook, and we continue to call her Sung Sook. I do not ask her why she changed her name. A year later, as her husband takes me to the airport to fly back to Baltimore after I spent six pregnant weeks in Seoul, he tells me that Sung Sook's mother never approved of their wedding or marriage. Sung Sook moved out of her mother's house. Her brother kept the house and the inheritance.

That summer of 2015, I also meet her younger brother, Yong Chul. He calls me on my cell phone and tells me that we will have a meal with our cousins. Sung Sook is not invited. The cousins are the older siblings of Chung Ran, the children of my father's older sister (Komo). We meet in Komo's house. They offer me tea and melon, and as we sit, they ask me if I have met Chung Ran. I say "yes" and that answer is met with looks to each other. The older sister, Chung Sook, tells me that I have a cousin who lives just outside Baltimore City, the youngest son of my father's sister. On the walls of Komo's house are pictures with my father. Chung Sook beckons me to the wall. "This is when I met your father. He was at our mother's eightieth birthday party." My father and Komo are sitting in the center of all the relatives, our cousins, and their children. My father is barely smiling, his face looks strained. A whole network of relations that had been kept separate from us.

Vague memories surface. I am in graduate school. My father says on the phone to me something about having to make a trip to DC to meet his sister. He says that he does not want to go but that he has no other choice but to go. He will be away from home for a few days. He had told me stories of his sister and her husband, pervaded by betrayals: how her husband forced my father to work in his factory and did not support him to study. How my father did not have the money to cover tuition for Seoul National University, although he had received a top score on the national entrance exam. He knelt at the gate of the university with his head down, begging for extra coins from wealthier students. How, when my father reached the United States and began graduate school, he sent money back for his young cousin whom he cared for deeply. He sent the money to his sister. Later, he discovered that the young cousin endured terrible hardships, while his sister kept the money. At that time, my father's stories of his sister's betrayal were interwoven with the madness of our domestic life. I had become accustomed to thinking of all this as "my webs of incomprehension," always there, lurking in the corners, always there, in phone calls, a story crashing into an unrelated conversation.

When my sister comes to meet me in Seoul in the summer of 2015, I arrange a dinner with the cousins and a separate dinner with Chung Ran and our komo. Chung Ran hosts the dinner in an upscale Korean/Japanese restaurant. Komo has dementia and does not speak very much. As we chat, it is not clear to me that Komo is following the conversation. Chung Ran helps her eat. Suddenly, Komo speaks with great lucidity, looking at us with hard, focused eyes: "I want you know that my husband cared for your father very much. He bought your father clothes when your father traveled to the United States." She repeats this three times. I translate for my sister, whose face tenses up. I nod and say, "Yes, Komo. Thank you."

One year later, when I meet my cousin, our komo's youngest son, Hak Jin, who lives just outside Baltimore City, he throws a big feast. The older daughter, Chung Sook, is also in Maryland. Her younger daughter also lives in the suburbs and runs a bagel shop, while her older daughter practices law in New York. Their oldest deceased sister's son, a pastor in Columbia, Maryland, also arrives with his wife and children. Hak Jin is now a contractor for Verizon. He had immigrated to the United States as a manual laborer. He was working to lay the light-rail in Baltimore City when his foot was amputated in an occupational accident. He won an out-of-court settlement with his employer and bought a large house in an upper class neighborhood in the suburbs. Addressing all at the dining table, Hak Jin brings up a story of my father's visit for his mother's eightieth birthday. He suggests that my father had somewhat spoiled the mood of the party by talking of past betrayals. He says in a disparaging tone that my father could not "let go of the past." Directly addressing me, he asks, "How is your father?" I tell him that we are trying to have him move in with us but he refuses. That the children are all worried about him, even if he is sometimes difficult. He is, after all, our father. Hak Jin smirks. "Oh, yes," he says sarcastically, "you need to keep up with traditions." I find myself recoiling from his tone, and perhaps my tone changes as a result. "So, you're a professor at Johns Hopkins. You know about our aunt who went crazy. She was smart too. The smart ones always go crazy." One of my father's cousins who lives in the DC area was studying for her doctorate in biochemistry when she developed schizophrenia. I had learned in bits and pieces over the years that my father was sending money to this cousin. When I had just moved to Baltimore, my father asked me to find and meet his cousin, to take care of her. Although I asked him for an address, he never sent it to me. I normally downplay professional academic status, as I have learned it has nothing to do with whether one is a thinking being. But I answer somewhat impulsively and vengefully, "Yes, *tenured*." "What car do you drive?" Hak Jin asks. I shoot back curtly, "A BMW i3." He turns to his sister but seems to be addressing me, "Does she speak *saturi*?" Saturi is a Korean dialect. Against the sophistication and cosmopolitanism of Seoul, it marks one as coming from the countryside—a country bumpkin. It is a shaded insult. I pretend not to hear it, feeling dangerously close to participating in my father's revenge on the world. Chung Sook tries to smooth it over: "You know that Clara didn't learn Korean at home and is learning it now."

§

While I am in Seoul, my father puts me in touch with his closest friend, Professor Kim. They both majored in physics at Seoul National University, the first graduating class after the cease-fire; they are both from the North. Professor Kim recounted how he and my father would walk in the Bukchon neighborhood, "fantasizing about leaving Korea, about our lives in the United States." Their dream was to leave Korea, to get admission into graduate programs in physics in the United States, Europe, or Russia. When Professor Kim asked me about my language training at Seoul National University, I mentioned that I thought it was a pity that my father did not teach us Korean. He responded, "You have to understand your father, how betrayed he and all of us felt by Korea." He related to me how many of the physics students at SNU were refugees from the North. Although they had the top scores on the national exam and were admitted into the top university, they were living in circumstances of extreme deprivation. "Two-thirds of us had tuberculosis from being so terribly malnourished." Professor Kim himself lived in one room with nine relatives and did tutoring for a wealthier Southern family just so that he could have a space to study. Although SNU physics majors were supposedly the pride of the country, the South Korean state did nothing to address the material deprivation and basic living conditions of their students—particularly those from the North, who had fled with nothing and who were discriminated against, just for the fact of being from the North.

For my mother, however, the story was different. At least this is what I am able to understand now. The connection to the mother tongue was what she desired for her children. When I visit my father's house in Los Alamos, New Mexico, where we all grew up, I find my mother's photo album. Photos of her family, her sister, her brother. She is writing on the back of these in both Korean and English, sometimes with *hanja* script. I send a picture to Imo, a black-and-white photo of my mother at Clark University where she had started her studies. In her dormitory room, she is seated at her desk.

Above the desk hangs the South Korean flag, and just under it, in hanja script, the word "노력" (effort, or striving). Imo writes me back, translating the hanja for me, and saying that this has a very deep meaning in the context of the times. 노력 is an expression of her enmeshment in the project of the new South Korea, a nationalism that was carried in her educational aspirations but also in the aspirations for her children, for them to recognize themselves as part of this nation-building in which one's place in a wider field of kinship is crucial. It may have been that Korea for my mother went hand in hand with kinship as genealogy and generation. For my father, however, kinship and Korea cut against each other and made us a "nuclear family." We might see in our names the bitter compromise my mother made for the sake of conjugality. In a manner that resonates with dol lim ja, my siblings and I were all given the middle name of 영 (Young). Young binds us together as a generation. But, in Korean, it is half of a name. 영 needs to be paired with another complementary character to make a well-balanced name, a name with internal harmony. Instead, it is paired with our English names: Clara, Andrew, Alysia, Michael. Have we lived with amputated names? Or did Young find a new route for complementarity among the siblings?

§

It was Korea's betrayal and Korea's future that made us—the children—inherit Korean in a particular way. Through overhearing phone conversations, mom and dad saying in the phone to a relative, "그니까 . . . ," through hearing the codeswitching that our parents did to "shield" us from their fights, even though we knew from the angry shouts or the tense silence at the dinner table that something was just not right. Inheriting Korean was to inherit the ways in which betrayal and aspiration cut into each other, the competing impulses of children as revenge on the world or children as born into genealogy and nation, of separations and connections. Our lives in English were colored by this inheritance of Korean, of Korea.

Starting when I was just eight or nine years old, my father said he would pay me five cents for every grammatical error I could find in his physics papers. *The* equation, not *an* equation. A difference, not *the* difference. Subject, verb, object . . . , experimental data, imploding plasma shell . . . I earned two dollars over a long period of time, which I carefully saved in a piggy bank. At the school bake sale, I bought a two-layer cake with pink frosting and a maraschino cherry, bringing it home, so pleased that I had bought a treat to share with the family. My father opened the box and closed it with disgust. With anger falling over his face, he growled, "Is this how you spend your money?"

When I was around six or seven, I took around an old tape recorder in the house, pretending to be a journalist. My mother is chopping vegetables at the counter. I'm sitting at the dinner table tape-recording. "Mom, what is the difference between a peanut and an almond?" My mom pretends not to hear me, or perhaps just is lost in her thoughts. I repeat the question, "Mom, what is the difference between a peanut and an almond?" "They taste different, and peanuts make peanut butter, you eat it with jelly." "But what is *really* the difference, Mom?" My mom chastises me, "Clara, there's a dictionary right next to you, just look it up." "But I want to hear what you think. I'm taping." "Look it up. Do you always have to take that tape recorder around?" What was it that I was trying to do, I now ask myself? Was I testing the limits of our life in English, testing *her* through tests of dictionary definitions? Or simply being an irritating child? Later that night, I discover the tape recorder turned on just outside the bathroom door, where my sister, twin brother, and I were taking a bath. My mother had been recording our chatter, and

somehow, even then, I remember taking solace in that fact—
that our chatter was so precious as to be recorded. When my
mother fell ill, I searched for the recording of my back and
forth with my mother. I would do anything to hear her voice
again. I had kept the cassette tape in a decorative tin box,
wrapped in a coral-colored raw silk handkerchief that my
mother gave me, and hid it in the back of a dresser drawer.
It was my "time capsule." But when I played the tape, it was
a recording of mine and my siblings' bathtub chatter. Mom
must have used the same tape and recorded our chatter over
the "interview." Perhaps in this gesture, I can hear her voice.
Although I did not know it, I am learning what it is to be an
anthropologist.

My father is a widower now for over twenty years. He is
old. My siblings and I hire a helper who comes every day to
cook, clean. He has troubling getting up from bed. He can't
remember things well. He does not eat well, so is frail and
thin. He does not want to live with his children, fearing himself to be a burden but also fearing the loss of himself—he
says to me, when I urge him to move in with me, my husband, and our daughter Ella: "You know, I like to do my crazy
things." He is proud that I am giving talks at Seoul National
University but then says I should ask the Physics Department
to invite him to give a talk. "But can't you just come to Seoul
with me to meet your nieces and nephews, your sister?" I ask
him. "But after all this time, I need to show something."
I do not know if he will set foot on the peninsula again.

When we speak on FaceTime to my father, my daughter
Ella points to my father, calling him *haraboji*, much to my
father's delight, words in Korean that I never uttered as a
child. He wants her to have a future in Korean; he wants her
to travel to Korea, for the relatives and his friend Professor
Kim to meet her. She is going to Seoul this summer to meet
her cousins, aunts, uncles, grand-aunts and -uncles, and her

nieces and nephews. Her learning Korean with me, our future in kinship, might be that memory of the loss of a world. That is, the most quotidian and the most natural of actions—Ella learning words, wording the world—has been born into her mother's, her aunt's (my sister's), her grandfather's, and all our relatives' labors to be in kinship again with each other. We might say that birth and the feminine provide here a route to the reinhabitation of a world. Ella will find her own voice in this kinship, in Korean—her own struggles that I can neither predict nor attempt to predetermine. This is perhaps the promise of the child, her reanimation of language in the finding of a voice.

Interlude 2
Homeward Bound

Learning Korean might be one route to claiming anew a place in genealogy. Yet, that place is permeated with betrayals by nation and by kin, betrayals that I too have found myself voicing in new contexts but also repudiating. In this sense, learning Korean might be understood as a second inheritance, in which "the step into adulthood is not established by continuing to grow naturally, but requires one's interventions in one's own life, making it one's own" (Cavell 2008, 53). Cavell describes adulthood as a "process of decision, call it the conversion of possibilities into actualities. This is the moment philosophers might view, or project, as consent to the society of one's predecessors" (53). How does consent appear in and as the immigrant; how does one inherit the condition of immigrancy?

In closing his masterful work on Vietnam and memories of war, Viet Thanh Nguyen brings us into two scenes of war, two pulses of memory—one embedded, or folded into, the other. The first is the scene of return, of paying respects to his father's father in his homeland. While his father's father is buried in his homeland, neither his father nor Nguyen himself, as refugees, will have that fate. When Nguyen arrives to pay respects, however, he discovers that his father's father is not buried in the mausoleum that was shared with his father's mother. Ten years earlier, he was buried in a muddy field, far from the living, such that sometime in the future his bones will be cleaned and reburied, closer to the living. The unearthing, cleaning, and the reburial of bones presents a picture of inheritance of war not as transmission but of the labor of bringing the dead home. Yet, homeland, here, appears through the paternal line. As Nguyen remarks, it is not the "country of origin" but rather "the village where one's father is born and where one's father was buried" (Nguyen 2016, 301). And Nguyen places himself within this paternal line through a contest between fathers and sons over the right to know one's past:

> As for my father, it is pointless to ask him about the past. His relationship to the past is to muffle it, at least in my presence. Although I have visited his homeland, I have never visited my own origin, the town where I was born, because he has forbidden it. More than once he has said to me, "You can never go back there!" Too many people will remember him and persecute me, or so he believes. . . . And while I have disobeyed my father in many things, I cannot in this one thing. The paternal injunction is too strong, the specter of the unknown past is too unsettling. (303)

Placing oneself in the paternal line, as the son of a father, seems to invoke past as commemoration and the utterly unknown.

Yet, embedded in this scene of fathers and sons is a fleeting domestic scene of a son and a mother, in which the child seems to be pressed upon by overwhelming knowledge that he cannot quite make out. Nguyen's mother comes home from a twelve-hour workday in the family-run supermarket:

> She asked me if I wanted to go for a drive with her, without my father. Perhaps I was eleven or twelve, maybe younger. We drove silently through the night, the window rolled down for the cool breeze. The radio was off. My parents never listened to radio in the car. She would not speak to me, or perhaps she did and I did not listen or do not recall. Even if she did speak to me, I do not know what I would have said. We drove into the hills in silence and then we returned home. Perhaps this was her way of reaching out to me, the boy who had lost his mother tongue, or who had cut it off in favor of his adopted tongue. (301)

Nguyen's mother's is ill. Her memory and body are "vanishing." Now, he cannot ask her what she was thinking then. Nguyen closes this scene by emphasizing that she counts in the public narrative of war: "She will not be counted as one of war's casualties, but what else do you call someone who lost her country, her wealth, her family, her parents, her daughter, and her peace of mind because of the war" (301). But I would like to pause before making the leap to secure the mother's story within the public sphere. Unlike the scene of commemoration in which the son must either submit to or transgress the father's vision of war and kinship, in the scene with the mother, we see a child learning to endure silence, which is also a learning to reinhabit a domestic marked by war. In this way, we see how inheriting the war is not simply the inheritance of the event of war or a traumatic past but rather the inheritance of the different impulses born in kinship.

The impulses born in the father and the mother signifi-
cantly complicate discussions of immigration and racialization with respect to the category of Asian American. Consider
David Eng and Shinhee Han's notion of "racial melancholia," which they define as an "unresolved process that might
usefully describe the compromised immigration and assimilation of Asian Americans into the national fabric" (Eng
and Han 2019). Writing against a dominant psychological
framework in which the "Asian" immigrant family is seen in
terms of a clash of two cultures, one of which (the Asian) is
pathologized, Eng and Han argue that racialization defines
their predicament as immigrant: that is, the demand to
achieve whiteness and the inevitable failure of that achievement for Asians because of their perpetual status as foreign (see also Cheng 2001). Resonant with Abraham and
Torok's theory of transgenerational trauma (see Introduction), Eng and Han argue that the relations of first- and second-
generation immigrants are a negotiation between mourning
and melancholia. The first generation bears the wounds of
loss in the unconscious that are inherited by the second generation. Yet, this second generation re-enacts these wounds
through their own "attempts to assimilate and negotiate the
American dream" (Eng and Han 2019, 49; see also Okazaki
and Abelmann 2018).

Within this context, the loss of the relation to the mother
tongue is understood as the traumatic coercion of whiteness.
Take their discussion of a patient Nelson, a Japanese American college student suffering from depression. When Nelson
was a small child, a schoolteacher admonished his mother
to speak English to him in the home rather than Japanese.
The mother then began to speak to Nelson only in "broken
English," while Nelson was shamed by his teacher for his
mispronunciation of English words. Eng and Han see Nelson's
depression as tied into this loss of intimacy with his mother,

the loss of a "safe, nurturing, and familiar language to the young child (Japanese)" (Eng and Han 2019, 54). They see his decision to become an English major as a dramatization of this struggle to master assimilation.

While immigrants are no doubt subject to the violent effects of the US politics of racialization, an overbearing focus on assimilation and the coercion of whiteness risks casting the predicament of the immigrant and the inheritance of war and displacement as wholly defined by racial politics in the United States.[1] That is, it risks completely eclipsing the various politics that are voiced within the family and how the contest over these politics involves the struggle to authorize the real. In this sense, cutting the mother tongue from oneself may not only be a consequence of the assimilation politics of the host country but may also relate to the betrayal by one's "home" country. It may also be an expression of the effort to find *one's own* language.

Remarking on autobiography and voice in Cavell's thought, Naoko Saito describes inheritance as "one of 'stealing'—in the sense both of the child's voice being stolen (the 'theft of selfhood, psychic annihilation' as he is moulded by or incorporated into the received language) and the child stealing his voice from his parents (appropriating words for himself, against their apparently settled meaning in the vocabulary he inherits). . . . In this sense inheriting language from one's elders involves a process of translation as treason" (Saito 2009, 260). Let me return again to Nguyen and to the different impulses of the mother and the father that we see in his description. Through living the pain of "cutting off my mother tongue," he learns the language of fiction, a language that takes both the paternal injunction and the mother's silence as somehow his own. And in that labor of self-making, he writes, "I was bilingual again" (Nguyen 2017, 307).

PART III
The Kids

Old Age

Our father drives slowly, cautiously. But his reactions are less decisive, and he ends up braking or swerving too late. Nearly two years ago, he got into a serious car accident. The car was totaled. The airbags released, saving his life. He was taken by ambulance to the St. Vincent Hospital emergency room in Santa Fe, where he was promptly cleared for discharge. But the impact lingers. His body aches all over. He cannot get up from the couch. He has to show up in court. He tries to wage a battle, adamant that he is not at fault. His friend Ron, a retired physicist, is roped into my father's defensiveness. He drives him to the crash site. They take pictures of the tire marks on the road. My father never mentions the accident to me. He calls my twin brother, Andy. Andy calls my sister, Alyse. Alyse calls me. Andy flies out to New Mexico to meet a lawyer. The judge restricts our father's driver's license. His insurance premiums increase. He is beside himself. He forgets to take his insulin, forgets to eat. He doesn't take his phone calls. My sister fears that he may have taken his life with an insulin overdose. We panic. I end up calling the Los Alamos police from Baltimore to do a wellness check on our father.

My sister Alyse is a psychiatrist. She thinks that our father is in a spiral of uncontrolled diabetes, leading to confusion, the confusion both intensifying the depression as well as blurring our ability to assess his cognitive decline due to early stages of dementia. She sets up a visiting nurse to visit our father twice a week. Deena, the nurse, calls Alyse. She says that our father is so thin and frail, so malnourished, that we may want to think of hospice. He tells Deena that he does not want to live anymore. My sister flies out to New Mexico, beginning her nearly monthly trips to oversee his care. She wants him to live. She throws out the cookies, Snickers bars, and Coca-Cola piled up on the counter. She gets him an electronic calendar. It displays the day of the week, the time, and whether it is daytime or nighttime in huge, white print. It sits next to our father's pill box and printed instructions of when to take his medications. When she is not visiting him, she calls him each afternoon that Deena is not there, reminding our father to take his medicines, watching him inject his insulin over video chat.

§

Alyse emails my twin brother Andy and me. She's at her wit's end, even as it dawns on her that our father may simply be making his peace with dying. These responsibilities need to be shared. She cannot bear this all by herself. I fly out to visit our father for four days. Ella is six months old and stays in Baltimore with my husband Maarten. Our father still cannot acknowledge that Ella exists. He talks incessantly of my sister's son—his only grandson—Thomas, who is two months older than Ella. Thomas's pictures cover the refrigerator door. I find the pictures of Ella that my sister had given to our father buried under a pile of junk mail on the kitchen counter. When I talk to Ella on the video chat, my father sits next to me. Ella is crawling under the table, smiling and giggling. "She's already crawling. Thomas is not crawling yet," he says, surprised. He turns away, uninterested, "She looks aggressive," projecting on Ella the contempt he has for her mother. It will not be until he meets Ella, and Ella smiles at him and hands him a book to read, that he would call Ella "such a gentle soul" and claim her as his granddaughter, calling her simply, "the baby." Returning from New Mexico, however, I text my sister. She texts me back, "It's ok if you want to step back from this [from our father's care]."

§

I have always said that my siblings are the reason that I am sane. But I've also asked myself what can be exacted in the name of staying sane, like letting my sister bear the brunt of our father's care because she wants to protect me.

Two Families

"Clara Beara," a babysitter with long wavy brown hair sings out to me. She is sitting on top of the jungle gym, where Alyse and I hung ourselves upside down by the knees, where Andy did loops on the rings. I had run around to the front lawn, upset about something. She tries to coax me to come back to the jungle gym where Andy and I sometimes flung ourselves from the top to the grass below, in contest not with each other but with gravity, to fall and be okay at the end. Among Alyse, Andy, and me, nicknames proliferated. Andy and Alyse called each other "Bo." I called Alyse "Los" when I learned the German word for "wrong." Alyse and Andy call me "Bear."

The proliferating nicknames, however, were inscrutable to our mother, father, and older brother. They referred to us collectively as "the kids." An unruly bunch, we were caught up in trying to collectively decipher the enigma of our older brother's and our parents' moods but also often completely absorbed in the play worlds we made with each other—in sofa pillows and blankets made into forts for ourselves and our stuffed animals or in games such as "Milligon" that we made up as we rode in circles on our bikes in the driveway.

The other Hahn family in town spells their name "the German way" with an extra *h*, a spelling that my father scoffs at. They have three sons; their backyard is kitty-corner to ours. So we can stand at the corner of our backyards and invite each other to come over and play. They also have an Andrew. But their Andrew is a virtuoso pianist and violinist. His piano playing wafts into our home. Our mother points to the window in our living room, "Listen to Andrew practice! You should practice too!" But we are somehow more disorganized and disobedient. Alyse, Andy, and I walk home from school together. We throw down our backpacks and turn on the TV. Alyse makes us snacks with whatever ingredients are around, always adding a peculiar twist just for fun: strawberry pink frosting spread on sliced white bread and cooled in the freezer for three minutes; popcorn mixed with a can of sardines; a tortilla microwaved with an American cheese single and butter. Our mother calls us from work to check in on us in the afternoons. Alyse usually answers but tells Andy and me before she picks up to turn down the volume on the TV. I do not remember doing much homework.

When our older brother Mike comes home after tennis or soccer practice, he sits in the green La-Z-Boy rocking chair, eats a bowl of cereal, and watches TV while flipping through Ken Hom's *Complete Chinese Cookbook*. Before our parents come home from work, Mike assigns us chores, areas that we are responsible for tidying up: Clara—counter;

Andy—floor; Alyse—dishes. He makes us ice cream shakes as a reward. Sometimes Mike allows himself to be dragged into our play, like when he lets my sister and I paint eye shadow on his eyelids. But much of the time, Mike tries to orchestrate the play. He's the master of ceremonies of me and my twin brother's birthday party, corralling us to play musical chairs and pin the tail on the donkey. He snatches us as we walk down the hallway toward the bathroom and locks us in the closet until we beg for mercy. He has us ride on his shoulders, and we scream with fear and delight. We are eager to please Mike, perhaps just because he is our big brother and we look up to him, but also because his changing moods can fill us with dread.

What does Mike know that we don't know? What has he refused to relate to us? At dinner, we sit around the oval table in birth order, counterclockwise. I always sit opposite of Mike. Alyse sits next to him. My twin brother sits next to me. Our mother sits at my right. Our father sits at Andy's left. I try to avoid looking at the dour expression on Mike's face but end up staring at him. Catching my eyes, he gruffly remarks to me, "And you, with the halo above your head. Like you're such a little angel." Mike voices his frustration and upset to our mother but not to our father. He wants his driver's license; he sulks in the house, "Well, because *someone* is not letting me get my driver's license . . ." Our mother would answer just by saying his name, "Mi*chael.*" When he and our mother bickered, I sometimes echoed one-liners from TV shows, "Can't we all just get along?" Perhaps because Mike had a deeper knowledge of the threatening undercurrents of this daily bickering, he found his little sister's canned, repetitive statements to be particularly irritating.

Our mother is in the kitchen, holding the phone in her hand, threatening to call the police. Mike puts himself between our mother and father, arms outstretched, his head

going back and forth between them. Our father takes Mike
to the garage. Later, Mike is made to put on his winter jacket.
It is nighttime. Our father tells Mike that he should go to the
police station and tell him that he is not wanted by his parents. My sister, twin brother, and I are standing with our
mother at the back of the hallway, watching. Our mother
whispers to us that if we misbehave, this will happen to us
next. Mike is in his bedroom. We open the door. We want
to console him. He yells at us, "Get out!" And so we retreat
back to my twin brother's room and worry about Mike together, separated from him by a wall.

§

I have often thought that our family life was marked by two
different biographies: our older brother inhabited and grew
up in a different family than the one my twin brother, sister,
and I grew up in. Our mother fell ill the summer before Mike
left home for college; my sister, twin brother, and I remained
and took care of our mother for another six years. Our growing up consisted of learning the daily labor of nursing, physical therapy, occupational therapy. We learn to administer
medicines, clean wounds, and how to prevent pressure sores.
We are also in the vortex of our father's emotions. But now
I'm unsure of this narrative. I realize now that each of us
struggled with two biographies: trying to just be kids, even
though affliction had shifted the normal.

Mike wanted to defer college for a year, but our father in-
sisted that he go. That first year, Mike records his voice on
tape cassettes and mails them back home. We play the tapes
for our mother. He describes the pink-red terracotta shingles
lining the building roofs at Stanford, the friends he is meeting, the classes he is taking. His voice breaks up with grief.
Like my twin brother, sister, and me, he holds onto the fiction of one biography with college friends and another with
his family. When he moves to graduate school at Harvard,

he scrupulously saves his grad student stipend and buys plane tickets to Boston for my sister, twin brother, and me. It is the first time I have been on an airplane and the first time I've been farther than Colorado. He takes us to a U2 concert in Foxboro Stadium. We eat lobster in a restaurant. We go to the top of the Hancock Building and look at the view. Mike made it possible for us to be "just kids" by taking us out of our home. But he was disappointed we could only inhabit this momentarily, as if that fiction wasn't already entwined with the fact that we were not and could not be just kids— that our normal grew out of affliction. Much later, when we are all "adults," Mike says to us in a fit of frustration, "Why can't we just be *normal*?! I just want us to be *normal*."

German

Our father wanted us all to learn German. He said that German is the language of Enlightenment science and Romantic philosophy. With German, we could become either poets or scientists. The bookshelves in the hallway of our house are filled with works from Goethe, Schiller, Brecht, Mann, and Nietzsche, in German. But also the works of Tolstoy, Gogol, and Solzhenitsyn, some volumes of which are in Russian. As a student at Seoul National University, our father studied German, Russian, and English in the hopes of ending up in one of those countries for his doctoral studies and in the hopes of leaving Korea. The physics students were better philosophers than the philosophy students, he says, we read Nietzsche together, sitting in circles on the campus lawn.

As the oldest child, Mike started learning German first. Then Alyse, Andy, and I began in middle school with Mrs. Harrison, a descendant of Pennsylvania Germans. She brings bratwurst to class and stollen at the holidays. The sweet temperament that she projects is punctured now and again by her stern rapping of a ruler on the table, "Listen!" she shrieks in English. In high school, though, we study with Frau Pedersen. She has a doctorate in German literature. Living in Northern New Mexico, she has no place to teach but high schools. Frau Pedersen introduces us to Sturm und Drang through the works of young Goethe and the poetry of Schiller and asks us to contemplate the Blaue Blume in Novalis's *Heinrich von Ofterdingen*, the doppelgänger in E.T.A. Hoffmann's *Der Sandmann*, and the dark transformation of Gregor in Kafka's *Die Verwandlung*. She tries to have us absorb the violence of mankind on itself through Werner Herzog's film *The Enigma of Kasper Hauser*. I am not quite sure how deeply I was able to absorb her teaching, but at the time, the themes of longing, the strangeness and doubled nature of everyday life, and the blurring of dreams, song, poetry, and story seem viscerally significant, though I could not articulate how or why. These themes resonated with our classmates too, who become our closest friends. We write notes to each other in our *Tagebuch* (diary) that we have to keep as part of class. One entry for ourselves, another entry for our friends. Our entries to each other become more and more elaborate, with sketches, origami, inserted pages made the night before detail the most petty but significant concerns—our crushes on a classmate or a spat with a mutual friend. Our friends show up at my and my sister's bedroom window at night. We escape through our window for a joyride in one of their parents' cars.

As my sister, twin brother, and I learn German, it becomes a language of our child world, a world that simultaneously shields us from and helps us endure what had become an intensifying sense of chaos in our home. Our talk is peppered by *jawohl, genau, ausgezeichnet, natürlich, ein bisschen, wieviel Uhr ist es?, noch einmal, langweilig, weltschmerz*. We reiterate to each other strange sayings that appear in our Ger-

man textbooks, such as, "Wenn man ein Radi gut schnei-
den kann, kann man auch gut tanzen." We crack jokes, speak
ironically, and intersperse German. When one of us eats
ravenously, we say, "ja, sie/er isst nicht, sie/er frisst!" When
things seem like they cannot get any worse at home, we exclaim, "Das ist genug!" Or, "Jawohl, genug ist genug." Or,
"Das ist nicht möglich!" As we banter back and forth, our
father laughs and says he has no idea what we are saying.

Today we still respond to each other with this German
twist: Alyse is hanging up the phone with me, "Ok, talk
später." It is as if the German words we learned carry the experience of the chaos of our home life. Perhaps these words
themselves bear witness to the catastrophe in our domestic
and, in their use, we somehow are showing that we survived.
Yet, German also bears witness to our father's dream to land
in a completely new world, to separate himself from Korea.
Maybe this is why our father never got irritated at our inde-
cipherable and at times utterly bizarre talk. Perhaps he too
sensed how, within the scene of affliction, it kept our domestic alive.

Five Sticks

I'm sick. Doubled over and vomiting. I had eaten a whole jar
of kimchi and drank the vinegar juice. I try to quell the pain
by eating a bowl of cottage cheese. But the pain and nausea
does not stop. My father is livid at my stupidity. Who the hell
eats a whole jar of kimchi in one go?! Days go by. I keep vomiting and walk doubled over, even as my father screams at
me, "Stand up straight!" Then suddenly, the pain stops, my
appetite returns. I'm relieved. I wolf down a cold bowl of
naengmyeon. But, as another week goes by, I start to notice
my belly swelling and each step I take, I think I hear a swish-
ing sound. I say to myself that I am imagining it. I go with

my sister and twin brother to our violin/viola lessons with our teacher, Kay Newnam. We are preparing for my and my twin brother's senior recital, a recital performed upon graduating high school. It is supposed to be a celebration. My sister has returned from Princeton. She will play a Dvořák trio with me and Andy. When Kay sees me, she asks if I would like to lie down on the couch in her studio while Alyse and Andy practice. I don't object, easing into the couch with relief. That night the pain returns, but this time it is accompanied by voices—shrill voices that pelt out words I can't quite discern; deep bellowing voices that indistinguishably laugh or cry; whispering voices that sound like the scuffling feet of mice.

I somehow wake up lucid but begin vomiting again. After my sister fights with him, my father finally allows me to see the pediatrician, Dr. Blossom. He has me lie down on the examining table, pushes on my abdomen and releases. The pain is overwhelming. He says I need to get abdominal x-rays. I do not remember much more of what happens next. A bearded surgeon with glasses is looking at the x-rays in the examining room, pointing, "This is her small intestine." My father is not there. I'm in the operating room. They are sticking IVs in my arms. The nurse asks me, "Sweetie, is your sister 18 years old?" "Yes. I'm 17."

I wake up. A nurse is pushing the hospital bed down the hall through double doors. Alyse is holding my hand. My throat hurts, there's something rough inside it. A tube is coming out of my nose. My first words are, "Shiiiitttt. Fucking shit." Alyse is telling me, "Sshhhhh. Don't say that. Ssssh-hhh." The nurse says to my sister, "She can say it, let her say what she needs to say." The surgeon visits me in my hospital room: "I worked in Vietnam as a surgeon during the war and I hadn't seen anything like this since then, till you showed up." The nurse gingerly broaches the issue of child abuse and

neglect, "You know that this could be seen as abuse . . ."
I bark back at her, "*Don't* try break us *apart*." My sister and
twin brother visit me every day. My violin teacher comes with
flowers. A popular high school student who is shadowing
doctors on rounds in the hospital visits my room, hearing that
I was sick. I had never met him before. His face is golden
brown and framed by golden locks. He says that he hopes I
feel better soon. Mike calls me, "What the hell is happening over there?!" His voice is trembling. I tell him that Dad
didn't believe I was sick. I spend nearly two weeks in the hospital. The nurses clean the open wound on my abdomen,
where a drain has been placed. Because of the abscess
formation, necrosis of the appendix and part of the small
intestine, the surgeon cannot stitch up the wound. I watch
television and the greenish-blackish liquid drain out of me
through the NG tube.

My father does not visit me in the hospital. Though, when
I am discharged and waiting outside, he picks me up. Luck-
ily, having gotten her driver's license, Alyse is driving and he
sits in the passenger seat. I can disappear in the backseat. He
says nothing on the ride back home. Every day, my sister
cleans out the open wound on my belly with Q-tips, lightly
patting it afterward with gauze dipped in iodine solution and
replacing the dressing, using the medical supplies we have
for our mother's care. I only discover then that my sister had
signed the paperwork to have me operated on, and in some
small-town way, the hospital accepted that she became my
legal guardian.

A few weeks later, when I regain some strength, Alyse,
Andy, and I rehearse the trio that we will play together at the
recital. We are sitting in front of our music stands in the main
hall at Fuller Lodge. I've lost nearly twenty pounds; skeletal,
I'm struggling to play. I stop. Furiously striking my bow on
the stand with each word, I scream, "Why—did—he—do—

this—to—me?!" I regain my senses and apologize to our teacher Kay. She tells us, release the rage into the music. Our recital is tinged with defiance—I'm still alive.

§

Our father repeated to us this saying: "One stick on its own breaks easily, but five sticks together don't break." For my father, "five sticks together" means sustaining mutual dependencies within a hierarchy. The eldest have achievements first, then the youngest follow. The eldest bear the burden of carving the path for the youngest. The youngest bear the burden of showing their gratitude for this path to the eldest. This hierarchy is both comforting and suffocating. I'm comforted that my sister will always beat me in tennis and that she steps in to make hard decisions for the family, fights for her role as the guardian of my twin brother and me. But I feel suffocated when I am placed above her in seating for orchestra and my father calls the high school music teacher to place me under her, because there is an order to our family life. I have to swallow feelings of frustration when I'm told that the only reason I've been able to accomplish anything is because of the path carved by the older siblings. I try to block out the sense that my sister views me as a threat to her existence— that I sometimes figure to her as a voracious animal that would gobble up and lay claim to everything before it; that my sister would feel compelled to see me as murderous, a variation on the narrative my father seeded in our family.

My twin brother diffuses this murderousness. He jokes that I was "found under a rock," bending the lethality into the absurd. Andy is always the one whose near preternatural sense of the absurd sutures the cracks among the siblings. When my sister and older brother have a terrible fight and do not speak for a year, Andy brings them together for drinks at a bar in Berkeley, cracks jokes that they both laugh at, and they begin to speak to each other again, what Mike calls "the

Kofi Annan Peace Accords." When Andy and Alyse are visiting me in Cambridge, we bump into my doctoral advisor,
Arthur Kleinman. Arthur praises us with a wry question,
"What happened to the other siblings who didn't do as well
as you all?" Without missing a beat, Andy quips, "Yeah. We
drowned 'em." My sister and I nearly expect him to make us
laugh each time we see him. He jokes about it: "The pressure! The pressure!" But sometimes Andy goes "radio silent"
as my sister and I say. He stops answering his emails or his
phone, momentarily withdrawing from the back and forth
of the siblings now and again.

   I repeat my father's saying to myself but as a narrative of
surviving the devastation in our domestic life. Had the siblings not had each other, it is difficult to imagine not having
lost our minds. But, perhaps all of us were threatened and
suffocated by the intensity of care, protection, and love that
made us into "the kids."

Different Continents

I'm on a flight to Paris, a stopover on the way to Nairobi,
where I will join a Princeton professor's research project on
indoor air quality in rural areas. Alyse has just graduated
from Princeton and has left with her boyfriend for Singapore,
where she will teach chemistry at Temasek Polytechnic. Andy
is staying in Princeton, where he is doing senior thesis research in a chemistry lab. Our mother has died five months
ago. We are now all on different continents. Tucked in the
book I am reading on the flight is a photo of myself and Alyse
that we took when we were hiking. Dressed in sweats and
raincoats, we are sitting on top of a large rock together. With
the photo in my hand, I cry all the way to Paris. The elderly
couple sitting next to me look at me with worried expressions.
They may have thought that the photo was of a relative who

had died. If the care for our mother required that we remain together and come together repeatedly, her death was a certain freedom from that care. It's as if we all just needed to disperse, to be on separate continents to claim that freedom. But the separation from my siblings, and particularly from my sister, felt like a death. It was not only the fact of being physically separated from each other but that our very world that we sustained with each other through the affliction might also be coming to an end.

When I am cleaning out the closet of my study in my house in Baltimore, I find a pack of letters from my sister that I have kept for the past twenty years. The summer that we all disperse to different continents, my sister and I begin to write and post letters to each other, and when we are able to, we send each other emails. I had forgotten that I kept these letters, transporting them between multiple moves, all these years.

Summer 1996. I am in Laikipia District, Kenya. The Princeton faculty is undertaking field research in a village located on a private game reserve. The host of the main house of the game reserve is an elderly British man named Colin. His reading glasses sit atop his sweater-covered potbelly, held by a cord around his neck. He mocks the use of mefloquine to prevent malaria, saying that the quinine from his gin and tonics does the same, but at least they are enjoyable. He says it will be hard for me to learn Kiswahili because I'm still mastering English. A British ecologist directs the research center on the game reserve. His steely blue eyes are pinpoints in his large ruddy face. He looks at me as he would a strange bug out of place. I follow around an evolutionary biology doctoral student and public policy masters student as they attempt to implement solar power cookstoves within a village on the game reserve. Women are using them as storage boxes. I write out impatient impressions to my sister, re-

calling anthropology professor Vincanne Adams's course on
critiques of development I had taken a semester before.

A letter from my sister finally arrives after a month. She
describes to me the apartment she is living in in Singapore,
the hawker stands where she eats cheap noodles with her
boyfriend, her fear that her hair is falling out from ingesting
too much MSG, her new roommates at the university where
she teaches, her students and the science experiments she de-
signs for them. I write her a letter, describing driving on dirt
roads, the visits to municipal health centers, hours photo-
copying sheaths of health records, broken microscopes, and
stolen solar panels that were used to maintain vaccine cold
chains. The letters are filled with description, moving from
Singapore to Nepal, where my sister volunteered and traveled
for another year after teaching in Singapore, and from rural
Laikipia back to Princeton and then back to Nairobi, where
I stayed for a year after graduation.

But woven into the descriptions is a restlessness in our
own relation with each other, with our father, with ourselves.
Our father is struggling with his declining authority over us.
We are struggling with the vulnerability that this decline ex-
poses. My sister begins a letter saying that she cannot stop
thinking of me and Dad, that she feels "haunted" by us. She
needs to be free of our father, who cannot bear that she has
a boyfriend. He repeatedly casts Alyse into the role of the victim, as if the boyfriend is constantly taking advantage of
her. He blames me for not telling him that she was moving
to Singapore with her boyfriend and thus participating in my
sister's "degradation." In another letter sent while she is in
Nepal, she apologizes for not responding to my letters for
months. She cannot bear to read the letters I am sending to
her, in which I detail our father's depression and alcoholism,
and his stoking of my twin brother Andy's insecurities. Now
that she is in Nepal, she wants to "really be abroad," to make

decisions on her own terms, apart from what is happening at home. She is going to be in a village for two months volunteering on a research project on infant and maternal mortality with an anthropologist, a colleague of Professor Adams. Her self-questioning is a questioning to me: Why work in Kenya if you have no relationship to that place? What is the point of studying anthropology if the jargon impedes you from truly thinking? Yet, in another letter, she describes in minute detail the interior of a Buddhist temple in Kathmandu. The chants fill her with calm. She writes that because she is rejecting our father's demands that she split up with her boyfriend, return to the United States, and apply to medical school, she now feels she must be absolutely decisive. Yet each decision is weighted with our father's rage and with a sense of responsibility that her decisions also affect me and my twin brother. She writes that she awoke that morning and was missing me so much that, even as she writes, she cannot stop crying.

§

During those two years that my sister and I live on different continents, I await each letter from my sister as if my life depended on it. It was the oxygen tank I needed when I was adrift in the sea. Yet I sometimes could not bear reading the letters when I received them, picking them up and putting them down for days. My head pounds as I read through the maze of tortured self-questioning. Dread washes over me as I catch small phrases here and there, alluding to fights with her boyfriend and her impulse to starve herself in response to them. My chest tightens as I receive letters that seem so utterly disconnected from the desires and fears I try to voice to her in my own letters. What is it about these letters that makes me confront the fact that my sister is a separate being, who nonetheless is also my reason for being alive?

I had a similar feeling with my twin brother Andy, before our mother died. It was a fleeting moment. We are preparing to apply for college. Each of us has to write personal essays for the application. My father insists on reading our essays. With his reading glasses on, he waits in the brown plaid La-Z-Boy rocking chair in the living room. I rattle off an essay quickly and I hope against hope that he won't use my own words against me. He says nothing, asking, "Where is Andrew's?" But Andy's words are stifled. He simply cannot write. Our father orders him to sit down and write; he lectures Andy in the living room, needling every insecurity that he can sense in my twin brother; he screams at him when he loses patience. He calls my sister on the phone. She is in her first year at Princeton. He tells her, "We are in crisis." I hear Alyse yelling at my father. Then, Alyse talks to Andy on the phone, trying to calm him down. She talks to me, "Dad is insane! But you've got to withstand this, bear." Our father yells at me, saying that it is my fault that Andy cannot write. I'm such a domineering presence. But, the more that my father berates all of us, throwing us all into an intensifying madness, Andy is further rendered mute, paralyzed. My father says that he will write Andy's essay. He sits down at the typewriter, humiliating my twin brother. Andy and I are in the bathroom, looking at each other in the mirror. We're silent. He's staring at me; I'm staring at him, his shocked and numbed face. A well of frustration surges up in me. I silently say to myself (to him), "Just write it out, damn it. Write anything!" I turn to him, grab his shoulders, and shake him hard, "Snap out of it! Snap out of it!" Andy just lets himself be shaken. His lifelessness is somehow my lifelessness, but I cannot make his words live. I am utterly helpless.

Butterfly

Mike is getting married. Alyse is now living in Berkeley. Andy in Los Angeles. I have just moved from Nairobi to Boston.

We all come together in Palo Alto, where Mike is in medical school. It is the first time we have all been together since our mother's funeral. Mike takes us on a wine tour through Napa Valley. The Han siblings together—we soak it up, revel in it. We stuff ourselves with cheese, bread, and olives. We make toasts to "good times" with wine, then port, then sake.

Mike had invited our father to the wedding. Our father obstinately refused. But the beauty of the day is a balm for Mike's burning disappointment. The wedding is at Auberge du Soleil. The view is stunning. The sky is bright blue. Chairs sit in tidy rows on a wide wood deck. Hills of vineyards lay upon grassy plains. A harpist plays. My sister and I are bridesmaids. My twin brother is the best man. Mike and his fiancée Virginia had arranged for a "secular humanist" justice of the peace to conduct the ceremony. My sister, twin brother, and I stand at Mike and Virginia's sides. The justice of the peace pours wine into two gold-colored cups. Both Mike and Virginia are to take a sip of wine from each of the cups. He holds up the first cup. This is the cup of happiness. They take their sips, thus committing themselves to a life together in happiness. When he holds up the next cup, the cup of sorrow, a large monarch butterfly alights on the cup's edge. It stays there, slowly beating its orange and black wings, as the justice of the peace brings down his arm in amazement.

We catch each other's eyes. We all immediately knew. Our mother is here. She is the butterfly. Mom, we knew you would come.

Crosshairs

Who is in Dad's crosshairs? For years, my sister is in the crosshairs. Our father is infuriated by the fact that she has a boyfriend. She does not speak directly to our father for several years. Then, my twin brother is in the crosshairs. Amid intense self-questioning, Andy takes leave from his doctoral training in chemistry and moves to Singapore to teach for a year. He too stops speaking to our father. For years in graduate school, I am the conduit between my father and my siblings. I call him every week to check in on him. He tells me that he has stopped drinking after reading Alyse's diary. He says that he felt pinpricks all over his body and that he was trembling. He had gone through alcohol withdrawal by himself. He tells me he has been losing weight. He saw the doctor. He has diabetes, but he cannot resist the peanut butter cookies and Snickers bars. He asks me how I am doing. My answer, as always, a tight-lipped, "Fine. Things are fine." I know that sooner or later, I too will be in the crosshairs.

Our joke about crosshairs, though, is one way to deflect the much more suffocating feeling that our father was only able to see his children as extensions of himself—his craving for revenge would be realized through his children. We (he) would prove "them"—Korea, his family, The Lab—all wrong through our (his) success. Anything that threatened our (his) realization of his craving was a threat. So, the very fact of our separateness was an internal threat to his existence. To spite us or discipline us into merging back into him, he would disown us, as if he were amputating a part of himself. But the threat of our separateness surfaced differently between the boys and girls of the family. With my sister and me, our father cast our sexuality and sexual future as a battleground between himself and another man. In this battle, the boyfriend was pillaging what was our father's to begin with. Or, perhaps more precisely, the boyfriend was pillaging our father, since there was no separation between our father and ourselves.

§

I am on the phone with my father. I tell my father that Maarten and I are going to get married. He stutters, "What?!"

Then, he recomposes himself, laughing, "So I need to buy you a white dress!" I'm dumbfounded. I tell him that we plan to get married in Cambridge, Massachusetts, and that I've already looked into renting a Spanish tapas restaurant for the reception. He says, "No, no. I will choose the place. I will invite your aunt from DC [our Komo] and we will have a big banquet in a Chinese restaurant." The fantasy becomes more and more outsized. "Okay, Dad, we'll see. We'll talk about the arrangements more," I say. A week goes by, I call my father. He now expresses hesitation. "I was thinking that if you get married, you need to do it right." I am not sure what this means. My sister writes me an obscure email, "Don't worry about it, bear. It will be fine." My father is ranting to my sister about my getting married, "Clara is with a Dutch drug dealer!" I call my father. I lie. I tell him not to worry about the wedding. We're not going to do it after all.

A few months later, Maarten and I get married in the front patio of the three-decker house where I rent an apartment in Cambridge, Massachusetts. We invite close friends and mentors. Maarten and I allow ourselves to say a few words. I describe a picture of my mother. She's my age, in a dark dress with pleats, standing in front of a pond lined by reeds. Birds fly above her head. Her hands are folded together before her. Her face is calm but serious. Perhaps I intuited then that the sheer act of description keeps my mother alive to me.

Alyse had applied to be a twenty-four-hour justice of the peace. Standing on the front steps, she conducts the cere-mony. Maarten's father and mother give some words from their side of the family. I ask my advisor, Arthur Kleinman, if he could say a few words. I can tell he is a bit reluctant. He asks me repeatedly, "Are you sure you want me to speak?" I insist, and so he goes onto the steps to give us his blessing. Alyse offers her own words, opening with how Maarten won her over by making her sushi and ending by declaring, "I now pronounce you husband and wife!" At the reception, Mike steps in and gives the toast. As the orthopedic surgeon in the family, he jokes that it has been less than twenty-four hours since meeting Maarten, but "he has a strong handshake and no visible open sores."

A few weeks later, my father flies out to Cambridge to attend my graduation from Harvard. Maarten will accompany my father in the audience as I parade in regalia with my friends. At first, my father reacts to Maarten with a stony silence. But Maarten offers my father a goat cheese sandwich on fig and olive bread that he made as a snack. My father takes a bite and says, "Wow, that is really good." He eats the whole sandwich. A fragile peace has been restored.

But a few years later, my father boils over with rage again at the fact that I am with Maarten. This time, my twin brother, his wife, and their six-month-old baby drive down from Boston to Baltimore with my father. My sister flies to Baltimore from San Francisco. We were to spend Christmas together in Maarten's and my new house. During the car ride, however, our father grumbles incessantly about Maarten. My twin brother is at his wit's end. He throws my father's suitcase into the middle of the street in front of our house. My father refuses to come inside. When he finally does he sits without speaking and then says he wants to get a room in an airport hotel. My sister and I drop our father off. I'm stifling tears, as I think to myself: Dad is old. His rage can last a very long time. His rage may outlast his life, and this may be the last time I see him alive.

For five years I am not in contact with my father. My siblings tell me how he is doing. I am in Santiago, Chile, doing fieldwork. My sister comes to visit me. She meets my "twin soul" in La Pincoya. We have a huge feast with her extended family. We travel to Patagonia. I get tenure. My sister conveys the news to my father.

My father is visiting my sister in San Francisco. Maarten and I had just left a day earlier back to Baltimore because we did not want a confrontation with him. Before we leave, Maarten helps my sister set up an IKEA bookshelf with a desk, an IKEA hack. My father admires the bookshelves with built-in desk. My sister seizes the moment and says glowingly, "Maarten did it." My father responds, "He has some skills, doesn't he?" He says to her that we don't know how much he has suffered. He had to stop talking to me so I would come to my senses. He misses me. My sister relays this to me on the phone. I see him the next time we visit San Francisco, in my twin brother's house in Palo Alto. My father says that I "look the same but a bit different." But then, it is as if nothing has happened. He tells me about the physics paper he is working on. It is both eerie and comforting that the last five years seem to not have existed. Eerie and comforting that goat cheese sandwiches and IKEA hacks have the potential to bring us back together.

§

Perhaps it is all too easy for my siblings and me to cast ourselves against our father, to take him as the foil to ourselves. In doing so, we can't see how the fact of separateness seems to also be a threat to *us*, as "the kids." Because the battle over our separateness has taken place on the terrain of our sexuality, my sister and I tend to take this terrain as a site of struggle among ourselves, as if intimacy with another is a threat to this "we."

Alyse needs me to get along with her boyfriend. But I simply cannot stand one after the other of them. I'm overly protective of my sister. I growl and snap at her boyfriends, a rabid dog on a leash. When one tries to demonstrate his acumen on the politics of poverty, I bash him down, rattling off one study after another. When my sister voices her insecurities about their relationship, I only stoke them by pointing out that boyfriend's "fatal" flaws. My overprotection of her is mixed with the fear that I'll be left alone. When I first meet Maarten, my sister at first outright rejects him. She is infuriated: I wasn't supposed to find a boyfriend, I was supposed to be there for *her*. Later, she says to me, "You're not going to have children until I have them, right?" It suffocates me. When our twin brother excitedly and fearfully announces to our father, my sister, and me that he and his partner Moon are expecting their first child, my sister and I react horribly. How absorbed were we within our own need for "the kids" that our niece's existence would not be a cause for celebration but a threat?

§

But perhaps making our father into that foil also allows us to evade our continuing compulsion to protect him, to bear unbearable emotions so that he continues to be part of our lives. We have lived many years with the dread that our father might die alone. If he rejected all of us at once, what would we do? That the crosshairs rotate means that he will be accompanied in his old age by one, and by extension by us all, "the kids." When I was a graduate student and in the depths of depression, I talked to a therapist who, after the first session, replied to me, "Your father is either evil or insane." She sat in her green armchair, her short, gray, curled hair framing her wrinkled face. Her penciled eyebrows and stiff forest green turtleneck conveying her conviction in every single one of the words she uttered. I was taken aback, and while my impulse was to defend my father against her—against the world—I simply left the room. Our father is not a monster. He is not evil. The insanity does not reside within my father as much as it resides in the world that we inhabit with him.

Cousins, Grandkids

Every weekend, my sister's son Thomas and Ella see each other on video chat. Thomas sings "Wheels on the Bus" or

"Hello, Ella" while plucking strings on his ukulele. Ella dances. Thomas reads a book, Ella points out excitedly, "Frog! Caterpillar!" She runs to her toys and shows Thomas a stuffed elephant, saying with the utmost seriousness while nodding her head, "Elephant, elephant." She asks my sister to do a somersault, "imosomersault?" We're now drawn into their play. When we video chat with my twin brother, Andy's partner Moon teaches Ella how to address her cousins Darcy and Yuna: "Say Darcy 언니, say Yuna 언니." 언니 (ŏnni) or "older sister" marks out her female cousins as older than her. But, a few days later, as Ella is falling off to sleep for the night, she says, "Bye Darcy 언니. Bye Yuna 언니. Bye 할아버지 언니 [grandfather older sister]. Bye Thomas 언니. Bye imo 언니 [aunt older sister]. Bye Uncle Andy 언니." It only dawns on me a few weeks later that Ella is not attaching 언니 to the names of the children across the street—our neighbors with whom she plays nearly every day—but only to her kin. How did she learn the boundaries of kinship? The shared gestures, expressions, tones of voice, the way we relate to each other— somehow she is piecing together our and her relatedness. It feels like we are witnessing a rediscovery of kinship. "The kids" are displaced to our kids, our father and mother's grandkids.

§

Spring. Our father's dog Elmo, a squat, barrel-bodied beagle, has just died. Elmo had a herniated disk, and over the course of a week, his hind legs became paralyzed. Because he could not walk, he could not use the bathroom, and he developed a urinary tract infection. The vet advises my father that it would be most humane to put Elmo to sleep. Elmo's paralysis coincides with a visit from my sister, her husband, and her son Thomas. Alyse helps our father take Elmo to the vet and is with him when Elmo dies. Our father keeps repeating, "Elmo was such a good dog." But he also wants another dog, perhaps because he knows that a dog's company may help keep home alive. I spend hours browsing adoption and shelter websites, send out emails to beagle rescues and sanctuaries. We finally find a four-year-old beagle for our father, but he suddenly decides he does not want it. He says he wants a puppy. I express some concern to my father. Puppies are unpredictable and energetic; they could jump on him and make him fall down. But he says that one of us will take the dog when he dies. Kids love dogs, he says. Perhaps leaving the dog to his grandkids is part of our father's way of leaving the world, as much as it is part of staying in it. If the dog makes home alive, then the dog's move to us can extend home to his grandchildren. Andy flies out to New Mexico. He takes our father to a dog shelter in Santa Fe. They find a small, mellow, one-year-old dog whom they name Kirby.

Summer. Our father has fallen off the couch a few times and has not been able to get up off the floor. Andy has installed grip holds throughout the house. The household help that we have contracted is visiting at irregular times during the day and night, to make sure our father is okay. When I call our father, he tells me that getting old is very hard. He says that he would like my twin brother, my sister, and me to all "come home." He says he wants to see his grandchildren all together—to have the house chock-full of kids again. We'll have a barbecue, he says, and watch the kids run around in the grass. I sense that our father's wish to see his grandkids happily play together and do utterly surprising little things is part of his preparation for death, that which he shares with us. Catastrophe displaced home for all of us. Yet in the image of a house chock-full of his grandkids, perhaps we see home momentarily shimmering in our father's words.

Interlude 3
Siblings and the Scene of Inheritance

In what way does the sibling complicate the notion of the intergeneration? My siblings have appeared throughout these chapters out of the simple fact that my existence is entangled with theirs. They are those with whom I have learned language and world, those with whom I have found and lost voice. Catastrophe is inherited through the chatter and play of children with each other, the creation of their own as-if worlds, their jealousies and rages with each other. These small ways that the child makes a world with her siblings moves thinking on the child from the order of law and contract to the details of and in everyday life. And yet, even as the sibling relation is a central vehicle to theorize inheritance in both psychoanalysis and anthropology, this mode of attentiveness through the give and take of siblings is, for the most part, completely eclipsed in the literature.

Take, for example, psychoanalyst Juliet Mitchell's discussion of the sibling relation as the hinge point through which the mother-child "pair" moves into the "many" of the group (Mitchell 2003). Departing from Winnicott and Klein, she sees the infant as identifying not just with the mother but with everything it sees: "so before it has a discrete 'I' (or ego) it has many 'I's' out there in the rocks and stones and trees which roll round in the earth's diurnal course with the many people it perceives" (Mitchell 2014, 5). Yet, as Mitchell further argues, even as the infant takes in this multiplicity, human dependence focuses on the mother-baby pair until it is disrupted by the arrival of a new baby. With the arrival of the new baby, the mother then pushes the toddler away from the family and toward the peer group. Mitchell sees this repudiation by the mother, and the substitution of the toddler by the new infant, in terms of "sibling trauma," an experience of annihilation or death "on someone else taking its place and all which that place and its emerging sense of individual identity signified" (8). This murderousness, paired with incestuous loving, must be socialized to go on living together. The play of the impulses of murder and incest seen within the structure of the Oedipus complex are now deflected into the "social group" or the dynamics among siblings. The primacy of the mother, in terms of offering a picture of human dependence, crowds out the multiplicity within the infant—of those many "I's" out there. This picture of dependence on the mother also seems to give rise to the notion of a unique place in the world, of individual identity, one threatened by the sibling.

We can return to Lacan's discussion of Antigone to see how the sibling appears in psychoanalysis not as a threat to unique identity but rather as she who bears witness to the uniqueness of being. Antigone says in justification of her defiance of the laws of the city, "If I had lost a husband in this way, I could have taken another, and even if I had lost a child with my husband, I could have had another child with another husband. But it concerned my brother, born of the same father and the same mother" (Lacan 1992, 255). Lacan remarks, "The Greek term that expresses the joining of one-self to a brother or sister recurs throughout the play, and it appears right away in the first line when Antigone is speaking to Ismene. Now that Antigone's mother and father are hidden away in Hades, there is no possibility of another brother ever being born" (255). Thus, this specific conjoining of the brother and the sister is irreplaceable. Rather than see the sibling as replacing the self through his birth, the death of the sibling is the death of a part of oneself. In Lacan's discussion of Antigone, the inheritance of language revolves around this axis of the sibling relation. For, through bearing witness to the uniqueness of being of her brother, Antigone inherits the laws of the city and transgresses them. Yet, Lacan's conception of language as being subject to the order of law crucially differs from a conception of language that takes the child seriously: as learning words through projecting them into new contexts. That is, siblings play with words stolen from adults and project those words into their own make-believe worlds. Through this play, they may find their own voice.

Children's play with words with each other, the creation of a make-believe world, raises a profound question as to what picture of inheritance is being imagined. That is, Antigone gives us a picture of inheritance as *who inherits*: she emerges as a subject through inheriting the laws of the city and her transgression of them. But the make-believe worlds created by children as they play with and project words into new contexts may give us a picture of inheritance as *what inherits*: that is, words themselves may bear witness to violence.

In a perceptive commentary on Nayanika Mookherjee's ethnography of the public memories of rape that occurred during the Bangladesh War (Mookherjee 2015), Swayam Bagaria asks if memory can be embedded within language. Contrasting Alton Becker's notion of lingual memory with the archive, Bagaria asks how language can be made complicit in bearing part of the memory of the violated women "even and especially because ultimately there can be no neat or straightforward communication of it" (Bagaria 2017). That is, women's utterances that draw from the oral-folkloric cachet not only are a recycling of past usages but rather leave a residue of experience on the word, born from the unique occurrence of the utterance. In this way, words bear witness to violence, but in a way that is recalcitrant to its inscription within the archive.

Let me return to the German language that my siblings and I dwelled in as we created a make-believe world. Speaking German with each other not only helped to contain the muteness ushered forth by a devastated domestic but also fashioned a different domestic that pulsed with life. As adults, these German words are normally interspersed in our talk with each other. If memory can reside in language, if words can bear the residue of experience, German words, for my siblings and me, bear not only the residue of that experience with death, dying, and madness but also the traces of that domestic created through those words. The picture of inheritance here emerges as an intimate history of the language of the domestic.

In studies of kinship, particular sibling relations are crucial to conceiving inheritance within the order of law and contract. The mother's brother, for instance, is a pivotal figure in theories of descent. In this way, the sibling relation itself is absorbed within preoccupations with genealogy (Alber, Coe, and Thelen 2013). In her ethnography of Malay kinship, however, Janet Carsten moves away from this preoccupation with law and contract to the ways in which siblings are staked in our lives. As she remarks, "In fact the form of the question in Malay: *berapa beradik?*, does not mean 'how many siblings *have* you,' but how many siblings *are* you.

The answer is given by the number that make up the complete set, rather than dividing that set and placing oneself in opposition to the other members. Once again the individual is conceived as constituted by her siblings" (Carsten 1997, 103).

Carsten evokes this existential nature of siblings again when relating a memory of her mother as a young woman: "Standing on the platform [for the train], she suddenly had the feeling that something was wrong at home. For no obvious or explicable reason, instead of taking her intended train, she took a different one—traveling in the opposite direction— and went directly home. On arrival, she discovered that her brother, to whom she was extremely close, had just received a diagnosis of leukemia. He died just a few weeks later and, as the manner in which Ruth told of these events made clear, her life from then on was irrevocably changed" (Carsten 2013, 245). The illness of her brother comes to the mother in the form of a premonition, perhaps speaking to the mysterious ways in which siblings are existentially part of each other.

Yet, it is precisely because siblings are part of us that we also learn separateness—that while you are staked in me, necessary for my existence, you are also a separate being for whom I am at times emptied of help. Inheritance as seen through the sibling relation reveals how play and make-believe worlds bear the marks of devastation of the world, but it also reveals just how precarious a shared world is, dependent on these flesh-and-blood others.

PART IV
Mother Tongue

Alyse has arranged a long-term caretaker for our father. While at first begrudgingly accepting the help, he comes to look forward to Lucy's daily visits. She watches him take his medications, cooks, and cleans. She spends time with him and sometimes apart from him, when he wants to be left alone but reassured by her presence. She calls Alyse. "Your father wants to go to Korea." He had asked Lucy to take him to the bank so he could buy traveler's checks. Alyse calls me. Does he really want to go? Will he change his mind? Can we afford multiple canceled tickets and rebooking tickets as he wavers? But, then again, how much time does Dad have left? It is time. We need to take him to Korea.

We will go for one week. It feels impulsive or, rather, like something is compelling us to take our father, despite a mistrust in our father's decisiveness. I write to the relatives: Imo and Kyung Mi; Chung Ran to arrange to see our komo; Sung Sook. I say, "Good news, we are taking our father to Korea . . ." Imo writes back, "You daughters [my sister and I] are magnificent for taking your father back to his hometown soil [고향 땅] where he has not been for fifty years. Clara, your Korean is getting so good. It is so important that you can speak in your mother tongue." Chung Ran writes back, "How is your father's physical condition? He must be healthy enough to travel to Korea?" She relates to me that komo had shoulder surgery last February and since then had suffered two strokes. She has been moved from the nursing home to a long-term-stay hospital for the elderly. The strokes had left her unable to speak, to swallow, and to move. Chung Ran writes that komo will have to receive a nasogastric tube to receive liquid nutrition. She says, "When Uncle comes and if Mom is able to endure/survive until then, it would be good if they can meet." Sung Sook writes, "Yes, we can meet, and let me know what food your father wants to eat." I write to Professor Kim, my father's friend from Seoul National University. I write to the chair of the Department of Physics at Seoul National University to see if we can arrange a tour for my father. As I write, it dawns on me that this is the first and the last time our father will be in Korea. Our komo is dying. Our father needs to say "goodbye" to his sister. But he also needs to say "goodbye" to all of his relatives, to his friends, to Korea.

Mother Tongue

The first week of November. The middle of the semester. I am teaching a course called "Korean War." We read on the counterinsurgency war in Jeju, the use of emergency laws during the US occupation of South Korea, anticommunist violence, the politics of commemoration, the student vanguard of 4.19 and the democracy movements in the 1980s. When I tell my father that I am teaching this course, he says, as a half-joke, that he could talk to my students. Yet, bits and pieces of my father's and mother's displacement are woven into the course. Our classroom discussions become woven into the days leading up to and after the trip to Seoul with my father.

But the travel to Seoul also revealed our father's deteriorating condition. Our father first arrives to San Francisco to stay with Alyse for a few days. Alyse tells me that he was limping coming off the plane. He spends entire days lying on the sofa, exhausted. I text Kyung Mi to see if she can help us rent a wheelchair while in Seoul; we become anxious that the travel itself might push our father into a health crisis. Alyse and our father fly together from San Francisco. I fly directly from DC to Seoul. We are staying in an apartment-hotel in Yeouido, close to where our imo lives. Our father can barely walk. He needs the wheelchair. He is occasionally disoriented. He asks us repeatedly, "Where are we again?" "We are in Seoul." "Oh, yes." The first night, he looks out the large glass windows with a view over highways, skyscrapers, and Yeouido Park. He says, "Seoul is scary."

The first night we arrive to Seoul, our father finds that he cannot speak Korean, nor can he understand Korean well when it is spoken to him. The next morning, however, we are picked up by Chung Ran. She takes us to see Komo. Komo is in a hospital for the elderly in Gangnam District. A large, airy meeting area with floor-to-ceiling windows greets us as we come off the elevator and walk into the hospital floor. My sister and I sit on yellow and blue poufs. Our father sits in the wheelchair. Chung Ran goes into the room that her mother shares with five other patients. A nurse is suctioning her mother's mouth. We wait.

Finally, Komo comes to us, in a wheelchair pushed by Chung Ran. Komo is unable to move. She has a nasogastric tube. She cannot speak. Yet she looks at my father intently. Her eyes are piercing, just like our father's. Our father takes her hand in his. He is smiling, saying repeatedly, warmly, "옥희누나 숙종이 왔어 [Ok Hie big sister, Sook-Jong came]." He asks Chung Ran, "She cannot speak?" Chung Ran takes her mother's other hand, "Ŏmma, Uncle came. Can you say his name? You said it yesterday when I told him he was going to come visit from the United States. Sook-Jong, Sook-Jong." She turns to us, "Yesterday, she said the first words since the stroke. I told her Uncle would come. She said, 'Sook-Jong.'" She turns back to Komo, "Sook-Jong, Sook-Jong, hmmm, Ŏmma?" Our father tells Chung Ran, still holding his sister's hand, "It's okay. It's okay. I know what it is to be with someone who has brain damage." He is referring to our mother. He holds his sister's hand to his face. Is this how you were with our mother? Is this the love that we, as children, were hardly able to see? When we take our leave, our father asks to see the nurse in charge. He asks my sister and me to help him stand up. Bowing, he says, in English, "Thank you for taking such good care of my sister." Chung Ran thanks them. The nurses smile and bow.

As we drive back to the hotel in Yeouido, our father points to the Gangnam River. During the war, he and his brother, along with thousands of others, walked across the frozen Gangnam River in the winter, escaping from the North Korean Army's advance on Seoul. He says, "My mother had sewn me a winter coat; it was a thick coat and very warm. I was wearing it when I fell through the ice. I got out, but my coat was heavy with water. It was freezing. I kept walking."

§

When we meet the cousins on our father's side, the exile from family and the rancor among themselves cannot help but gain expression. But the rancor coexists with their memories of our father's care toward them and his own tender memories of them. Through these memories, it is as if we

are seeing a father made before us that we ourselves hoped
to remember.

We meet Sung Sook, her husband, children, and grandchildren in a family-run *naengmyeon jip* (noodle soup restaurant). Our father relies on me to translate for him, "You
look so well, Sung Sook. I left when you were a baby. Your
father should have never taken you to that movie theater; that
is where you got polio. I am so happy that you are married
and have children." Sung Sook responds with a reassuring
smile, "Yes, yes. Uncle, please have some more food."

A woman approaches our table. "Sung Sook ŏnni?" she
asks Sung Sook. They had not seen each other since they
were small children, when they lived together in a house near
Namsan. My father; my father's brother, his wife, and their
just-born daughter Sung Sook; his sister-in-law's sister, her
husband, and her daughter all lived in the same house upon
their return to Seoul from Busan after the ceasefire. The
woman is the daughter of our father's brother's wife's sister.
"I recognized your father," she said. "He looks exactly the
same." She tells us that our father babysat her and Sung
Sook: "He always made sure we ate." What is this mysterious force of kinship? How is it that, after fifty years and with
my father's return to Seoul, long-lost kin reappear to those
who remained?

Sung Sook takes us to her daughter's teahouse afterward
in Itaewon. She keeps telling our father in Korean, "You need
to eat to stay healthy, okay? We want you to come back again,
okay?"

The next evening, Komo's older daughter and son, Chung
Suk and Myung Jin, along with our father's older brother's
son Yong Chul, take us to a fish restaurant in Yeouido. Myung
Jin meets us in the lobby of the hotel. I barely recognize him.
He is dressed in a slick navy suit with sunglasses tucked into
the suit pocket, a navy fedora atop his head. He swivels

around on his shiny shoes, bowing to our father. Our father asks, "Who is this?" This question becomes a refrain through-out the evening. Chung Suk hugs our father. At the dinner table, she points to herself, "Chung Suk. I'm Chung Suk, Uncle." One moment, our father remembers: "Ah, Chung Suk-i, you were such a cute baby, such a cute little girl. You used to wait for me at the corner and ask me to carry you back home. I would give you my briefcase and put you on my back." Chung Suk, "Our Uncle was so warm and sweet." Our father responds, "Myung Jin, you were such a nice boy, so cute." Myung Jin smiles. He says to Yong Chul, "I am sorry that I could not respond to your letter after your father died. My wife was ill . . ." Yong Chul coughs, "No, no don't worry. That is in the past." The next moment, he points to Chung Suk and asks me, "Who is this?" Chung Suk names herself again. Our father says again that she was such a cute girl. Chung Suk spins these reiterations in different directions, re-vealing and emphasizing the hatred among her siblings. "Yes, Uncle. You always took care of me. You didn't even know Chung Ran, she wasn't born yet. You took care of *me*." Our father just nods. He says with a smile, "You all turned out just as I expected."

§

"When are we meeting Daemann?" Our father would ask us this question repeatedly when we arrive to Seoul. It strikes me now that when he speaks of his friend, Professor Dae-mann Kim, our father seems closest to what might be called "home." This friendship emerges again in a visit to the Phys-ics Department at Seoul National University. The chair of the department, Professor Heonsu Jeon, arranges a lunch and tour with two colleagues, one who works on particle physics and another who has the largest lab in the Physics Department. Our father is disoriented in this polished, pro-fessionalized academic environment; one that his daughter seems to navigate, if not with ease, then with adeptness. He wears his partial denture, but they keep slipping down, impeding his speech. My sister discreetly has him slip them out of his mouth, quickly folding them in a tissue and putting them in her purse. At lunch, he cannot seem to follow the conversation on grants and funding. He picks up a sugar pack and rips it open, the sugar falling on his lap. I quickly clean it up. He does it again. I move the sugar packs out of his reach. He holds the empty sugar pack in his hands, tearing it into tiny bits that litter his pants. Yet, when Professor Jeon begins to name some of his classmates asking if he remembers them, he becomes animated. He speaks of Daemann and their friend Young-Woo. He jokes that he never studied but nevertheless thought of himself as a genius. He describes how Young-Woo met his future wife.

We meet Professor Kim in a restaurant in Yeouido. Beer is served. We try to limit our father's drink, but he insists on drinking more. They talk, they laugh, they trade barbs—funny, pointed stories at each other. Our father tells the story of how Professor Kim had fallen in love from afar with a pretty student. How he pined after this woman. On campus one day, our father and his friend grabbed Professor Kim, pulling him into the bushes, only to push him into her when she passed by. Professor Kim could only bow and say to her, "I know your older brother." Our father laughs, "Who the hell says that to a woman he loves?" Professor Kim blushes. He turns to us and says that our father took himself very seriously. No one could tell a joke about him, except Professor Kim. Our father commanded a classmate who told a joke about him to get down on his knees and apologize. The classmate did so. "I will never forget that," says Professor Kim, laughing. They piece together how they became friends with their friend Young-Woo. Together they were called "the Trinity" by their classmates. The night goes on. We lose track of time. Our father is inhabiting his school days. Alyse and I are the guests.

§

Young-Gyung is my friend. She is an anthropologist who lives in Seoul. Her father, an esteemed academic and founder of an important literary magazine and editorial house, also comes from the North, the same place where my mother's family comes from.

On a hunch that our father might enjoy meeting her, I arrange coffee with Young-Gyung at the National Museum of Modern and Contemporary Art.

Somehow, Young-Gyung seems to evoke our father's childhood world in the North. The food, the smells. She tells my father, giving me a wink, that he should exercise every day and eat well, because "things could change very quickly, and you might be able to visit your 고향 [hometown] soon. But if you are too weak to come back, you will be very sad. That will be so sad." Our father laughs and nods. Till this day, he continues to ask me, "When is Young-Gyung coming to visit?"

§

The evening before our departure from Seoul, we have dinner with Imo, her husband, and their daughter Kyung Mi. By this time, our father is speaking in Korean. It is as if every day, the Korean language was being awakened in him, only to have it fluently expressed with our mother's sister. We arrive at their apartment building. Kyung Mi greets us in the lobby, escorting us up to the thirty-second floor of the building. The apartment door opens. Imo says, "Oohhhh," with delight. She greets our father with a big hug. Our father shakes Imo's husband's hand for the first time. Alyse and I help our father into a chair. As if he had rehearsed this moment several times before, our father says with tears in his eyes, his voice cracking, "I am sorry that I could not bring your sister back alive." Imo looks puzzled. Dad says again, "I am sorry that I could not bring your sister back alive." While Imo struggles to respond, I try to deflect the unease into niceties, saying, "It's okay, Dad."

Dad continues, "I have waited for this moment for so long, and now that it comes, I do not know how to begin. There are so many things to talk with you about. When their mother was dying [pointing to my sister and me], I held her hand and said that I would take care of the kids. So, she can leave. 'You can go. Go.'" (He says this in Korean.) He says, laughing with tears in his eyes, "And today I proved it. My daughters are here with me."

"Yes," says Imo, "you have beautiful children, children that did so well." She invites our father to the table for dinner. Her husband [Imo-bu] tries to move the conversation into the register of small talk of current events. He comments on the thawing of relations of the North and the South. "The younger generation wants reunification. They want this to end, but they don't understand history. When I was a child, the North Korean Army took every sack of rice we had. I will never forget that. And if there is reunification, what will happen to all the land in North Korea? There are families like your mother's [he looks at me] who lost their land and have a right to it. What will the government do with their right to property?" He asks me, "What do you think?" I try to move around the ideological commitments he voices, "Well, those might be good points, but I think that for the 이산 가족 'separated families,' there should be every effort to reunify them, if that is what they wish." He leans back in his chair and responds dryly, "But in one generation, the 이산 가족 won't exist anymore, and it just won't matter." "But they exist now," I quickly reply.

I look at my father. He glances at Imo-bu briefly, registering but not reacting to the violence of that remark. My father's

attention is drawn to Imo. She sits next to him. He tells her
again and again that he has bought two graves and will be
buried next to Mom. He gestures with his hands on the table,
"One grave here. The other grave next to it. A shared tombstone." Dad says that Imo's hands look like our mother's. She
moves her hands to her lap.

§

"I am sorry that I could not bring your sister back alive." My
father's words show how war and affliction, large and small
catastrophes, are of the same fabric, the same weave of a life.
The war never stopped for our father; it continued across the
terrain that spanned Korea and the United States. Our
mother's affliction, her death, and her burial in the United
States are also part of that war. The affliction that struck our
mother and our family meant that our mother's aspiration to
return to Korea could never be fulfilled and that her aspiration for her children to reweave the world of kinship would
only be realized after her death. Yet, in the return to Korea
and the meeting with Imo, our father acknowledged—for the
first time that I can remember—our mother's aspirations for
this continuity with kinship and for her children to inherit
Korea and Korean. After a lifetime of trying to separate
himself—and, by extension, his children—from Korea, our
father ceded his own desire to voice our mother's desire. Or
perhaps our mom found a way to voice herself through our
father's words.

§

Alyse and I talk in the bedroom of the hotel the night before
we leave Seoul. We are both shaken by the visit with Imo;
shaken by our father's deteriorating condition. Alyse says,
"Do you remember that TV show that we would watch when
we were kids, where the grandma is sewing a quilt and when
she finishes the quilt, she will die? So, every night the grand-

daughter comes down and undoes the quilt. I feel like we are making the quilt for Dad."

Is this what we are doing, helping you die? Is this what daughters do? All this time during the preparation to go to Seoul, we said to friends, relatives in Seoul, and to each other, "I'm going with my sister to Seoul. We are taking our father to Korea." But after his visit with Imo, I suddenly realize that he was and has been taking us to Korea too. Perhaps the route that our mother had hoped to have opened for us to Korea closed with her untimely death, but our father opened a different one. In preparing for death, our father took us to Korea and Korean. In caring for his preparations for death, in working through each detail, we were invited into a world devastated by loss, yet not annihilated: one in which simple love stories, friendships, babysitting, and moments of tenderness with a sick spouse and sister had kept words alive.

Disease

It was a stroke. Three weeks after our visit to Seoul.

Dad was found down on the floor of the family room, unable to speak or swallow, by Frank, the man who delivers Meals on Wheels to seniors in Los Alamos County. Lucy, the caregiver, arrives. She calls the ambulance. He is taken to Los Alamos Medical Center Emergency Room. Lucy is texting Alyse, Andy, and me. A chaotic scene unfolds of which we only get sporadic text updates. To get a head CT, the ER physician gives our father an exorbitant dose of Ativan for his age. He has had a minor stroke, but the sedation is so heavy that he is unable to be roused from sleep for several days. He is transferred to a hospital room. Andy flies in from San Francisco. He stays in the hospital room with our father, to be there when he wakes up; to be there if he does not. And, miraculously, he does.

Next, I fly in. Dad is being transferred to the only nursing home and rehabilitation center in Los Alamos County, Sombrillo. Because our father could hardly walk and was still having difficulty swallowing, in consultation with his primary care physician, we decide that this is the best route to take before returning back to his house. However, the conditions of the rehab center are abominable. The stench of urine burns the air. Patients sit in their wheelchairs in a dark activity room for hours, parked in front of whatever DVD is on hand to entertain them. The nursing staff is stretched thin. Although my father is diabetic, not once do they check his blood glucose. Medications are regularly given late. One of the intake nurses, trying to be friendly, asks my father, "I bet you like rice, huh." Laughing, she goes on to recount how her former boss loved rice, imitating a fake Chinese accent, "I love rice." Our father is assigned a small room to share with a very large man with dementia. The man is sexually aggressive to the nurses, grabbing them. He hears me talk and sings, "I hear a beautiful female voice." He lunges repeatedly at the curtain separating himself from my father. He says he wants to see my father undressed. I step in between him and my father. The man grabs me instead. Dad watches, unable to move.

I live in the facility with my father, sitting next to him in a chair all night, every night. I am too scared to leave him alone in this pit of hell. Each night, every two hours, the lights are turned on bright to change the roommate's wet diaper. My father is constantly awoken. He asks me repeatedly, "When can we leave? Are we leaving now?" I text Alyse and Andy with the details of this nightmarish situation, yet we all somehow are committed to the idea that Dad would benefit from physical therapy. So, I tell my father to try to endure, "No, Dad, we're trying to get as much physical therapy here as possible." But as the days go on, it dawns on me that I am doing all of the nursing care for my father and that the harm and danger of staying in the facility far outweighs any benefit from one thirty-minute session of physical therapy. I tell him one morning, "Dad, we're going to make a jailbreak. I'm taking you home." After I get my father's discharge papers, I explode with fury at the head nurse who tells me wryly, "Because we are so short-staffed, when patients come to the facility with relatives, we let them do the caregiving, so the nurses can take care of the patients without family." "Are you out of your mind?! How can you assume that relatives actually know how to take care of a sick person?!" "That didn't occur to me before, but we'll address that in our next training session." To continue is pointless. I file a formal complaint.

At home, Dad sleeps. He can only wake for meals and rapidly nods off again. Alyse takes over. I fly back to Baltimore. She stays with my father for two weeks, her husband and son joining her. Then I return again, this time with Maarten and Ella. My father's dog has a fear of men, except for my father whom he aggressively protects. He barks incessantly at Maarten, bites him, and manages to tackle Ella, knocking her over. My father begins to have visual hallucinations of a black dog in the house, ants crawling everywhere, and a grid-like pattern of holes peppering the walls. I take him to the ER. Ella is screaming, "I want to go too!" Maarten pulls her away from me. He is taken off the antidepressant. The hallucinations stop. Alyse returns for yet another two weeks. Her son Thomas is having massive temper tantrums. This rhythm is not sustainable. Andy, Alyse, and I begin to talk: because his only asset is his house and he has minimal savings, the only options are to return to a facility for Medicare patients, like Sombrillo, or to live with one of us and use the sale of his house to cover the costs of a full-time caregiver for as long as possible. There is no question. Dad needs to move in with one of us.

Fate

It was decided that Dad was to live with me, Maarten, and Ella in Baltimore. I am not sure how. A few reasons might be given to make all of this seem like a logical conclusion: First, Andy lives in the Bay Area and cannot afford a house that could accommodate Dad as well as his family. Second, Alyse lives in the Bay Area as well but her husband was unhappy with his job and was applying to work in Switzerland. They could be leaving for Switzerland. Our father cannot move there because he is dependent on Medicare. (They eventually did move). Third, Baltimore house prices are lower, so we could collectively afford a house with an in-law apartment, if we pooled our resources. Fourth, although Mike has economic resources far beyond our means, he is out of the picture as he is estranged from Dad.

But really, why me? What is this strange fate? I'm talking to Andy and Alyse, as we edge nearer to the decision that Dad will move to Baltimore. I say, "This will mean that I won't be able to do fieldwork, take a sabbatical year in Korea, for as long as he lives . . ." Andy says, "Wait, wait. If this means that you can't advance in your career, maybe we should rethink this whole plan." I say, "But how the hell would I be able to live with myself if I am doing fieldwork in Korea, while Dad is rotting in Sombrillo? It just doesn't make any sense. It's ethically dissonant, somehow just plain wrong."

I'm sitting in my office on campus—a small respite from the whirlwind—when it suddenly dawns on me. This whole time that I have been learning Korean, I have been telling myself that I am preparing for my next major field research project in Korea, to newly animate long-standing questions on care, violence, poverty, and health. But now I realize that my learning Korean was not for a professionalized form of fieldwork "over there" but for this: for my father to move in with me, to be the one who arranges his care and who cares for him, for me to be the witness to his dying, for Ella to be brought into his living and his dying and death. Was Korean simply my preparation to receive him, his death? And is this not what it is to live as an anthropologist? To be witness to this life and this death?

§

As Maarten and I begin to look at houses in Baltimore, however, I become increasingly distraught imagining our future house as a dying space. What will happen to Ella? I tell my friend Veena of my fears: how I had to live through my mother's illness, how I am afraid that Ella will be pulled into the knot of care, like I was. What will that do to her? Veena reminds me, "But the difference is that *you* are the parent to Ella, not your father. You can show her what it is to die surrounded by love and not by violence." But how would I achieve that love?

In February, at the beginning of the spring semester, we move to a new house with an in-law apartment. While Maarten does the disability renovations for my father's in-law apartment on the first floor and preps the space for an elevator between the first and second floors, I unpack our entire house and then proceed to unpack my father's belongings that Andy and Alyse sent by container. We barely sleep two hours a night for a week. My hands are so swollen and full of cuts, I am finding it difficult to write on the chalkboard when I give my undergraduate lectures. Maarten is so sore from the physical labor that he can barely move. Yet, one week after we move in, my father moves in. My sister accompanies him, later joined by her husband and her son.

The transition is rough. My father's initial excitement about being with family all the time seems to dissipate as Alyse returns back to San Francisco. Our household is brought into the political economy of home-based caregivers and care agencies that reflect the racialization of Baltimore City. A white nurse manager visits our house from a care agency. Most of the caregivers are Black. She says, "I like to make sure that they stay busy and not just check their phones." She says she will come for random, unpredictable "spot checks" on the caregivers. I recoil at the surveillance and the moralism. We begin interviews of private caregivers found through care.com. Each woman has a story. One grew up in Baltimore, was in a situation of domestic violence, and is now divorced. She took care of her mother until her death a few months ago; through this care, she found her calling. One is a high school math teacher from the Philippines. She is working in a nursing facility as a backup reliever but is applying for teaching positions in Baltimore City Public Schools. One is a physician from Honduras, who arrived with her young daughter several months before. She is studying for board exams to become licensed to practice in the United States and needs a temporary job.

We begin to cycle through several caregivers, trying to find the right fit. Many of the caregivers are accustomed to working in large facilities, handling several patients at a time. While this work experience may allow for some knowledge on dementia to accrue, it also can mean that the caregiver has a tendency to treat my father like an object to be parked at the café, to be ordered to sit down, to be ordered to take his medication. Alyse finds a care agency that has Korean caregivers. Initially, my father is very excited. His Korean begins to return to him; he tells stories of how he met our mother. But the caregivers have so little knowledge, experience, and motivation. As my father sinks back into silence, they are at a loss and simply encourage my father to sleep during the day—closing the curtains and turning off all the lights. His days and nights become confused.

Dad is clutching onto shards of independence that have already been lost. He says again and again that staying in our house is temporary. His friend Daemann had moved to his daughter's house on Long Island with his wife who also has dementia. Dad says that he will buy a house next door to his friend. At first, I try to reason with him, "But Dad, who will do your cooking, your cleaning? We don't have enough money to buy you a house and to pay for care." He says, "Alysia will manage my money." He becomes angry. Later, when he expresses this desire again, I stay within the fiction and acknowledge his desire with the simple, "Yes, we can work on that." And then, a shift occurs, he writes his friend Daemann, "I am planning to buy a house in the neighborhood where Clara lives." He tells Maarten, "I like this neighborhood. I will try to buy a house next to yours." We all support him by saying, "Yes, that sounds like a good idea."

My father's short-term memory and cognition fluctuate with his fatigue, his sleep patterns, his mood, the stability or unpredictability of his blood glucose levels. But overall, they slowly deteriorate. He needs me for short-term memory: whether he ate breakfast, if he talked to my sister on Face-Time that day, if he went to physical therapy, and so forth. I, in turn, try to create a predictable routine that secures habit for my father—dinner is followed by brushing teeth, bathroom, and a change into pajamas, for example—such that he is not overwhelmingly dependent on this short-term memory.

As I try to find caregivers, I'm caring for my father full-time and teaching full-time. This means: persuading my father to get up in the morning; changing his bedding, which is often soaking with urine, doing the laundry; showering;

helping him use the toilet and get dressed; checking his glucose, watching him take his medications, preparing his
breakfast; reminding him to eat; taking him to appointments;
preparing his lunch; encouraging him to do physical therapy exercises; trying to find readings that might interest him;
cleaning his apartment; persuading him to go upstairs for
dinner; helping him change into pajamas, convincing him
to use the toilet and brush his teeth before he goes to bed;
preparing lectures; running to class; responding to students'
questions; grading.

This is all done while Maarten and I also take care of Ella,
in which we both try to make sure that her mother does not
disappear into the care for her grandfather. Maarten and I
create an infrastructure of care for both my father and Ella
that is so solid, so predictable that its hard edges are palpa-
ble. I don't know how long we can do this, I think. Days and
nights are this domestic labor, peppered by unpredictable
bursts of venom from my father, "You were always such a selfish girl."

When I tell my sister how hard this care is, she tells me
that our father can handle being alone for long periods. "If
you want to go out for dinner, just leave him some dinner
on the table." She suggests that it may not be so important
to make sure our father changes into pajamas each and every
night. "*He* doesn't care." She is right. If left alone, he simply
would not care to change his clothes. However, isn't the addressee of the question really myself, not my father? Do I care
to make sure he is in pajamas, so he can tell night from day?
Do I care that he is accompanied in his meals, so he remembers to eat? Care is my attention to you that makes you
human to me and makes me human to myself. Yet, I can see
the darkness in care that my sister is pointing to in her criti-
cism: that care itself can blind you to another's desires, mak-

ing the other simply a mirror for oneself. With dementia, my father, my siblings, and I all have to tread the delicate lines of life and lethality in this care.[1]

§

In the throes of caregiving, Mom comes back to me in my dreams. We are in the house in New Mexico. She is sitting in the dark-green, high-backed wheelchair, hair cropped short, in a hospital gown, unable to speak. I am sitting next to her in the family room, holding her hand. I am not a small girl but an adult who is also the mother of Ella. Mom squeezes my hand. I look down at her hand, and then glance back at her face. She says my name, "Clara." "Mom, you woke up?" She gets up from the wheelchair. We are now in the kitchen. She is leaning against the yellow kitchen counter. Her hair is now in a bob, black and wavy. Her brown-rimmed glasses frame her face. She is wearing dark blue jeans, the ones she wore on the weekends. She holds onto the counter for balance as she walks. Her body is recovering from the long, long sleep. But how did you wake up, I ask myself, watching her walk slowly, hearing her talk. She tells me repeatedly, "I'm awake. I'm okay now." Suddenly, my father appears at an entrance to the kitchen. Or rather, I sense him behind me, standing next to the dark brown kitchen cabinets. I stand in front of Mom and scream, "Stay—away—from—her!" I open my eyes. Mom is alive. Momentary doubts. But didn't she die? The sleep slowly fades from me.

Evening Stories

My father begins to tell stories of childhood and war. He tells them in the evening as we're finishing dinner: "The last time I saw my mother, she had come down from the hill to see

me. I was with my older brother, protecting him from getting drafted into the North Korean Army. She showed me a
piece of US propaganda that she hid right here [he makes
the gesture of hiding a leaflet in undergarments]. I told her
not to worry, that the war would be over soon and that
we would all be together. But she knew, she was walking
up the hill, dabbing her eyes with her dress. The next day,
the Chinese army cut off the road to the hill and that was
the last time I saw my mother."

§

"See those chipmunks?" My father points to the chipmunks
running over the backyard patio outside. "When we were
kids, we used to take a grain of barley and wrap a string
around it. Then, we would pull the barley along the ground
and trap a chipmunk. We'd put the chipmunk into a small
wheel, and it would run and run and run in the wheel till it
got exhausted. How cruel we were. [Laughing.]"

§

Ella peels a mandarin orange for my father and hands it to
him, "Here haraboji." He laughs and says: "My grandfather
always had boxes of mandarin oranges. They came from
Japan. My mother's brothers went to Japan to study and they
always came back with mandarin oranges for grandfather.
But he never once shared them with any of us kids. He ate
them all himself."

§

"No one wanted to take grandfather in when the family got
dispersed. He was such a terrible man. He was in a neigh-
bor's house where my sister was hiding. He was sick and died
there. He was buried in the backyard. Then later, they dug
up his body and gave him a proper funeral." I ask, "When
did this happen?" "After the war, sometime." "But weren't
you already in the South? How did you know?" He doesn't
answer.

Dreamscape

As the caregivers encourage him to sleep all day, my father seems to be increasingly living in a dreamscape in which most conversations he has are in his dreams and not in his waking life.

I wake him from sleep to have dinner. He says that he saw his mother's face in his dream, that his mother keeps coming to him in his dreams. As we go up the elevator to the second floor for dinner, he looks down at his hands, "When I see my hands, I see my mother's hands. They look so similar."

The next evening, I am waking him again to go upstairs for dinner. He dreamed of his PhD thesis advisor, "He was such an awful man. I only have contempt for that SOB."

Yet, sometimes, these dreams take on lives of their own with others. He awakes and tells me he dreamed of a math textbook that he had as a student at Seoul National University, one that he had to sell in order to pay his way to the United States. "I almost had the name of the book in my dream, but then I woke up." When my students Sumin, Sojung, and Sahun come for dinner, my father shares with them the details of the book. With the students, he speaks fluently in Korean, telling them of his time as an undergraduate, as if he were in that time again. Through the back and forth, the students are able to find the book. And later, Sumin's sister arranges through a friend to buy the book in an antique bookstore in Tokyo and send it back to us. My father's dream materialized in holding this book in his hands. He says, "The book made it back home."

§

I'm carefully cutting my father's fingernails and toenails, kneeling on the ground, while he sits in a chair. He says this makes him remember what he promised to his mother:

"I said to her that I would be back and cut her fingernails for her. But I wasn't able to see her again."

§

My father shares his stories and dreams with me less and less each day. Now, he rarely speaks to me at dinnertime. If he wants something on the table, he just points to it. It is as if he has retreated into a cone of silence. This may be because of his exhaustion with me or with my exhaustion from the ceaselessness of household chores. This may also be the disease speaking. Or perhaps all this *is* the disease speaking. At the dinner table, only Ella seems to bring him out of the cone of silence.

What Ella Learns

Ella is two and a half when my father moves in with us.

My father needs to have his blood glucose checked in the morning and the evening. It is a few days after my father arrives to Baltimore. Ella is sitting at the table for breakfast. I say to my father that we need to check his blood glucose. He holds out his hand. I prick his finger and squeeze for a drop of blood. Ella's eyes are big and round with worry. She leans across the table, "Haraboji, are you okay?" She turns to me, "Is haraboji okay?" "He's okay, Ella. We're just checking his blood sugar."

She smiles at my father, makes funny faces. But my father just stares at her. Sometimes, he furrows his eyebrows, and it looks like he is angry. Other times, he opens his eyes wide and looks surprised. When he talks, she does not understand him. When she talks, he does not understand her. I become the translator between them. "What did he say?" "What did she say?"

My father sits at the head of the table. It's the easiest place for him to be seated. I had put Ella's seat next to my father's

seat. I sit next to Ella. Maarten sits across from Ella. One
night: Ella cries, "I want to sit in someone's lap." "Can't you
just sit in your chair?" "No!" She throws her food and laughs.
I have to bring her to the living room to "talk" about "sharing space." I ask her, "Don't you want to be nice?" With tears
rolling down her face, she cries, "Yes, I want to be nice!" She
manages to return to the table and finish her dinner. Another
night: Ella is playfully pretending to be a baby, rubbing her
eyes with her fists, saying "I'm a baby crying." My father,
almost always silent, suddenly sternly shouts at her, "Don't
do that!" She looks at me with a sad frown. She starts to cry.
Another night: My father tries to engage Ella, but he does so
by wiggling his index finger around her face. No one is
sure what he is trying to do. Ella looks confused. She looks
at me. I must also look confused. Ella starts crying. She tells
me later, "I'm scared of haraboji." I switch her chair with
mine. I sit next to my father. Ella sits on my other side. My
body blocks their direct interaction.

§

Slowly, Ella starts to take on my voice when she interacts with
haraboji. It is as if, in figuring out how to relate to him, she
needs to take on my words, my tone, my gestures:

"Haraboji, if you tap the chair like that, Dotty [our cat]
will scratch you. Don't tap, please."

"Haraboji, don't forget to eat."

"What are you doing, mama?" "What do you think I'm
doing?" "Taking haraboji's blood sugar. Ninety-four, that's
good."

"Here, haraboji," Ella pulls out my father's chair for him,
as he approaches the table.

§

Slowly, haraboji appears in her play. She grabs one of
my father's canes, walking around, saying, "I'm an old, old
man."

Slowly, she brings words together with impressions. We are driving back from preschool. Ella is looking out the window. She says, "I can hug haraboji. Haraboji can hug me. Sometimes haraboji kisses me. Sometimes haraboji doesn't eat much."

§

"Who is that?" Ella asks me. "Haraboji's nurse-friend," I reply. Ella recoils at many of the caregivers. They get into her face, forcing an intimacy with her and our family that does not exist. Others try to assume a parental role with her, telling her to finish her breakfast, not to yell, to listen to her mother. I try to protect her and cut them off mid-sentence, "Give her space." Each time a new caregiver comes to the house, Ella says, "I want to go to preschool." It's as if our home is not home for her, and school has become the source of her stability.

But, with other caregivers, she invites them into her world. "Will Mina play with me? I want to give Mina a hug." Then, through a stroke of luck, the world of the caregiver and her world become knit together. My colleague and friend's mother starts as the full-time caregiver of our father. Yumi's son Joongbin goes to the same preschool as Ella. I tell her, "Joongbin's halmoni [grandmother], Yumi's mom, is going to take care of haraboji." Ella is excited: "Will she play with me?" She sees Yumi's mom in the preschool. Jumping up and down, she exclaims, "Joongbin's halmoni is here, she is in our house. She is here, she is in our house!"

§

My father had to give up his dog upon moving to Baltimore. We promised to get him a new dog when he arrives. We get a puppy and call him Huchu. He is a black, fluffy ball of fur that keeps growing larger and larger. Although he looks like an innocuous Muppet, is calm, and rarely barks, Ella's home is again unsettled. She says, "Mama, why did we move to the new house?"

"Because haraboji got sick and had to move in with us."

"I want to move back to the old house. I don't like Huchu."

Again, she takes on the tone and gestures Maarten and I use with Huchu as if to assert her own fragile mastery, "Huchu, down!! Huchu, sit!! Huchu, leave it!!" He lays down, he sits, he leaves it. She says with happy wonder, "He listened to me!"

§

Dad caught a bad cold from me. He is very weak. He struggles to walk to the dinner table. I hold him firmly by the back of his pants, his legs buckling every few steps. He sits at the table. I serve him a bowl of chicken noodle soup. He is watching Ella. She is squirming. One minute, her knee is bent and foot resting on her chair. The next moment, she is trying to lean her head back onto my lap and eat lying down. "Ella, can you sit up?" I turn to my Dad, "Dad, don't forget to eat." I am eating dinner, watching him. He cannot seem to bring the spoon to his mouth. Perhaps he is leaning too far back in his chair. I get a small throw pillow and put it behind his back. He opens his mouth, as if anticipating the spoon. Yet his hand cannot move the spoon to his mouth. He tries to get the noodles on his spoon. "Dad, why don't you try using the chopsticks. They might be easier." "Yes." He tries again, but the noodles repeatedly fall off the chopsticks onto the floor. He's leaning far to the left. I get another pillow to tuck into his left side. Is his body unable to remember how to use chopsticks? I get a fork for him. I twist a small bunch on the fork to show him. He nods. He tries himself. He can't get the noodles on the fork. I make a small bunch again and lift it up to show him. He opens his mouth. He wants me to feed him. "No, Dad, I know you can do this yourself. Just put your hand here." I put his hand on the fork and wrap my hand around his. I lift the fork and his hand up to his mouth.

I look up to see Ella now seated between my father and Maarten. Ella is watching haraboji struggle to eat. The noodles falling on haraboji's left arm and trailing down onto the floor next to her. Her mother getting up from the table again and again to get the fallen noodles, clean haraboji's left arm with a dishtowel. Her mother says, "Don't worry about those noodles, Dad. I cleaned it up. Let's try again."

He is too weak to walk to the elevator to go back downstairs. His knees buckle. Maarten quickly brings a chair so he doesn't crumble onto the floor. I get the wheelchair. It's the first time that we have used it inside the house. With the wheelchair, there is not enough space in the elevator for anyone else. I close the door and send the elevator down with the remote control. Ella cries and screams, "I want to go down with haraboji!!" She repeats this again and again. I snap, "Stop it!" She stops, surprised, looking around for Huchu. Her mother never yells at her like that. She only yells at the dog like that. But Huchu is nowhere to be seen.

The next morning, Maarten, Ella, and I are in the car, going to the farmer's market. I am driving. Maarten is in the backseat next to Ella. Looking at the road, I start talking to Maarten: "Yesterday was really concerning—that he could not feed himself and that he actually wanted to be fed. It was the worst shape I have seen him in. If that becomes his normal state, I'm not sure how we are going to take care of him. He seems better today. He could come upstairs with the walker."

Ella: "Are you talking about haraboji?"

Surprised, I glance around, "Yes, we're talking about haraboji. He's doing better today."

At dinner that evening, Ella insists on sitting between my father and Maarten at the dinner table. My father is wearing his Boston Red Sox baseball cap. Ella says, "Can I see your haircut?" My father asks me, "What did she say?" "She wants to see your haircut." "Oh, you want to see my haircut." He lifts off his cap. Ella turns to me and Maarten, "Haraboji can still talk." My father's eyes open wide and he nods his head. Ella turns to me, "He says 'Yes,'" nodding her head. I turn to my father, "Dad, I think that Ella was worried about you." At dinner, the next night: "Haraboji can still talk." She looks at me for confirmation. "Yes, he can still talk." Ella: "He can still talk. And he can still hug." Ella seems to be sensing how fragile my father is; how one day, he might not be able to talk and he might not be able to hug. She is learning illness, learning dying.

§

It's dinnertime. Ella says, "I want my chair here." She moves my chair out of the way and pushes her toddler chair next to my father's. She then moves my plate to her placement; her plate to mine. "You want to sit there?" I ask. "Yes, next to haraboji." She is now sitting next to my father. We had gone for a walk in a small forest close to our house earlier that day. There, Ella points out a tree that had fallen down. "The tree is upside down," she says. I explain to her, "This is a tree that fell down. It got so big and so old that it had to fall to the ground, and its roots went up in the air." At dinner, Ella brings up the fallen tree or "the tree with the roots up." I demonstrate with two florets of broccoli and my hand. One floret is the treetop, the other the roots. My hand is the soil. "See, when it falls, the roots go up. And the tree lies on the soil and turns into the soil." Ella asks me, "What does the soil say to the tree?" I respond, "The soil says, 'We're so happy that you are with us. You can turn into soil, like us.'" Ella says, "Then the tree sleeps." "Yes," I respond. "It's like the tree with the crane," she says. She is weaving this story to another tree "story" that we discussed a few weeks before. Then, as we were driving to preschool, we saw a huge crane bringing down a section of a large oak tree. I said to Ella, "Look, they are taking down that tree!" She asked, "Why?" And as with the fallen tree, I said, "The tree was so old, it was time to come down. So, the crane helps the tree come down."

As we talk, my father is intently listening and watching. He understands we are talking death; he laughs with wonder at this child talk. Ella then turns to me and Maarten. With a slight question mark in her voice, she states, "This is family." She looks at all of us for confirmation. "Yes, this is family," we all laugh. She asks my father, "Haraboji, are you happy?" "Oh yes," says my father. We laugh again. What is it about this child's learning that can bring out the life in dying?

Epilogue
Seeing Like a Child

Ella's world is a child world. It is a small world. When she builds a rocket out of Legos, she does not say, "It's going to the moon." She says, "It's going to the farmer's market," a place that exists to her. When she lugs around my orange suitcase through the house, she says she is taking an airplane to "Russia," where her preschool teacher went to visit family for three weeks. Her world grows as she draws words together with things. In learning haraboji, Ella learns that family is a scene of fragility and dying but also one of happiness and love. All this is her inheritance. Yet, as witness to this learning, I am drawn to inherit anew, allowing her puzzles to give me puzzles, her open bewilderment to breathe life into my own.

In writing and readings these pages, I am struck by how the physicality of care is embodied so differently by the girls and boys of the family, such that the girls—who become women—name the violence in the domestic in ways that the boys do not. This naming of violence is seen in the agonizing emotions surrounding childbearing and the preparations for the death of a parent, as if women become midwives for this texture of life and death. I am also struck by how, throughout the text, my mother appears as very much alive: in the memory of her cool hands, the games she played with us, her small frustrations, her wavy black hair, her clothes, her words, her aspirations. And yet, the clear division between boys and girls, mother and father, falters as I see my siblings and parents bear impulses of both the masculine and the feminine. While my mother participated in what might be understood as a masculine imaginary of the South Korean nation, my father's fragments of memories and his rejection of a South Korea and North Korea evokes the feminine region of memory that resides at the boundary of nationalism. However, my mother's desire to sustain relatedness against and despite the corrosion of war and displacement can be contrasted to my father's insistent and violent authority to define the terms of belonging in the family, as if he could cut out our mother tongues before they had a chance to be born. Yet, in my father's last visit to Seoul, he channeled my mother's voice: to heal kinship relations wounded by war and displacement.

Indeed, there seems to be an interplay between the child's voice and the mother's voice, as if seeing like a child overlaps with, or somehow shades into, a region of the feminine. Here, rather than claim mastery over a narrative as in a contest between fathers and sons,[1] one reclaims membership in a form of life through attention to the small, the diminutive, the low—not as if one were returning from exile but as if one were discovering and transforming the terms of belonging where one already is.[2] As the child of my parents, and the mother of my child, this means inheriting Korea and Korean not as a question of identity between two different cultures but rather as learning kinship, illness, dying, and death. It means allowing myself to receive this world—marked as it is by war, migration, betrayal, and the loss of voice as much as it is by love and care—as my world.

In this way, seeing like a child draws close the relations between the generations, a fragile reinhabitation of everyday life. This body of writing is therefore not a testament to the continuity among the generations. It is a body through which these relations are reborn—relations that mark my anthropological thinking.

Acknowledgments

This book breathed life into me. Although it was simmering in the recesses of my soul, conversations with Andrew Brandel and our inspiring cowriting gave this book a body. Although we ultimately decided to allow our published words to travel apart, Andrew's conversations with me are borne out in every page of this book.

This book is written for my mother and father and for their granddaughter, Ella. If my book achieves anything, I hope that its words help sustain a weave that draws my parents and my daughter near to each other.

I have deep gratitude and admiration for Tom Lay at Fordham University Press and Bhrigupati Singh, my co-editor of the *Thinking from Elsewhere* series, who both were so deeply committed to seeing this book out in the world. Thank you for your unwavering support.

There are several colleagues and friends who have sustained my intellectual life and responded with such generosity to this project in all its iterations. Veena Das read the entire completed manuscript, as well as various parts of it as it was coming together. Heonik Kwon has been an inspiration and a source of encouragement. Thank you for inviting me to present part of my writing at the Korean Society for Cultural Anthropology meetings in Seoul, which was a wonderful opportunity to share these fragile thoughts. Hyang-Jin Jung at Seoul National University, Kim Taewoo at Kyung Hee University, and Bo Kyeong Seo at Yonsei University have invited me into rich intellectual communities in Seoul, for which I am so grateful. I hope with time to continue these conversations. Lotte Buch Segal, Tobie Meyer-Fong, Grégoire Hervouet-Zeiber, and Amy Krauss read the manuscript in fine detail and provided acute comments. Conversations with Diana Allan, João Biehl, Erin Chung, Angela Garcia, Naveeda Khan, Yumi Kim, Eduardo Kohn, Paola Marrati, Marjorie Murray, Michael Puett, and Lisa Stevenson have been a constant source of enrichment. I also presented part of this work at the Avoidance of Childhood workshop as part of the International Research Network (GDRI) "Forms of Life." Thank you in particular to Estelle Ferrarese and Sandra Laugier for ushering this network into existence. Parts of my writing appeared in a coauthored article with Andrew Brandel entitled "Genres of Witnessing: Narrative, Violence, Generations" that we prepared for a special issue of *Ethnos* edited by Lone Grøn and Lotte Meinert. I am grateful to Lone and Lotte, as well as to Helene Risør and Lotte Buch Segal, for the opportunities to present this writing at the American Anthropological Association meetings in 2015 and 2016. I also thank current and former graduate students, postdoctoral fellows, and faculty from the Anthropology Department and East Asian Studies Program at Johns Hopkins who participated in a book workshop held in October 2019 led by Richard Rechtman. IM Heung-soon, Sungman Koh, Monica Kim, Jaewon Chung, and Young-Gyung Paik participated in the workshop "Kinship, Gender and the State in the Shadow of War: The Korean War in Comparative Perspective" held at Johns Hopkins in February 2020 where I presented parts of the manuscript. Thank you for a magical, intense conversation that opened up new directions for engaging the absences, shadows, and destruction of war. Thanks in particular to Young-Gyung, who revived my father's talk of his 고향 before the dementia made it difficult for him to find words, and for being there to talk about pretty much everything related to Korean War, the partition, and life. Thank you all for doing all you can to sustain intellectual community.

Graduate students in the Anthropology Department at Johns Hopkins University also read and commented on parts of this manuscript and read the entire text. In particular, I thank the Methods Seminar, Fall Semester 2018—Zeynel Gül, Heba Islam, Kunal Joshi, Basab Mullik, and Sarah Roth—for giving very stimulating and insightful discussion of the manuscript, as well as Sojung Kim and Youjoung Kim who read the entire manuscript with such attentiveness.

My undergraduates in the course Korean War, taught in Fall 2018 and Fall 2019, read the manuscript and gave incisive comments. I am particularly grateful to William Engfer, Clara Leverenz, Katy Oh, and Tanya Wongvibulsin for sharing their thoughts on the manuscript. Thank you to graduate students Sojung Kim, Sumin Myung, Kayoung Kim, and Sahun Hong for creating a magical night for my father and bringing a long-lost book home. Thank you to Yoojin Madigan for your excellent and patient tutoring in the Korean language.

Since the time I entered graduate school, my advisor Arthur Kleinman had hoped I would do research in Korea. However, for over two decades, my intellectual life has been oriented to the issues of poverty, disease, and violence in Santiago, Chile. Then, Korea found me, through affliction and care in the domestic. Arthur, this book is a response to the care you have shown your student as she strives to make anthropology a way of life.

A deep thanks to the artist Park Daa Won who allowed her artwork *Now Here - Becoming* (2015) to grace the cover of this book. The resonance of her artwork and this writing is profound and moving, and I am so grateful for her generosity and for the vitality expressed in her painting.

My sister and brothers have taught me the existential perils and promises of kinship, made more acute with our father's illness. We need to thank ourselves for keeping our relations intact, despite the corrosions of disease. My husband Maarten has kept me sane throughout the period of my father's illness and care. Had it not been for your incredible endurance, patience, and ability to be organized, practical, and efficient in matters of household chores, our world would have fallen apart. Instead, we actually can and do have many moments of joy.

My mother 차정화 and father 한숙종 serendipitously met in the United States, both from families who fled from North to South during the war. Mom, although you died now twenty-three years ago, your breath is in my words. Today my father is losing his words to dementia. He does not know what day it is or where, geographically, he is. He lives with me, Maarten, and our daughter, Ella. In the fog of disorientation, my father retreats into silence. One evening after dinner, however, he heard Ella's voice in the next room. He spoke to me: "The little girl. When I hear her voice, I know where I am." Her small three-year-old voice existentially orienting him to a life in kinship. This book is dedicated to the relations between these generations.

Notes

Foreword

1. The publication of the English translation changes the verb *donner* to a noun, *The Gift of Death*.

Introduction

1. Literary models of trauma bear a similar impulse to organize experience within a coherent frame built around catastrophe as an event. The study of testimonial projects has shown how survivors attempt to reconcile the "disruptive" memories of catastrophic violence with the fabric of their lives and how these attempts at reconciliation are constantly failing (Langer 1991). The catastrophic event cannot be immediately assimilated. It is belated or split off, repressed by the self or by social institutions. Academics, psychiatrists, artists, and the public-at-large can bear witness to the survivors' symptoms of unassimilable experience and therefore transform trauma into what Cathy Caruth calls "unconscious historical testimony": "they have made the study of and response to trauma into a site of historical memory and have, conversely, revised our notions of what it means to remember

and to act around the imperative to respond to something that consistently resists conscious assimilation and awareness" (Caruth 2015, 2; see also Caruth 1996). Caruth suggests that there are both ethical and political stakes in "the persistent and renewed encounter with the urgency of the event," which entails transforming trauma into historical testimony within the public sphere (Caruth 2015, 2). See Crystal Mun-Hye Baik's *Reencounters: On the Korean War and Diasporic Memory Critique* (2020) for an extremely cogent critique of the postmemory and trauma literature from the perspective of those who have lived and inherited the Korean War. Baik makes the important point that postmemory studies presume that the catastrophic event resides in the past. However, the Korean War is an unfinished war and cannot be limited to the chronological time of 1950–1953. As she writes, "Refraining from describing the Korean War as an event that can be accessed or 'known' only through its invisible residues, I examine diverse manifestations that congeal as political, social, and affective formations seemingly removed from the context of war" (Baik 2020, 23).

2. Because Abraham and Torok assert, contra Freud and Lacan, that the ego is coherent, they tend to focus their efforts on the re-establishing of the ego over the unconscious and thus slide into psychology (Lane 1997). As we will see, Lacan directly challenges this notion of "recovery" of happiness and, like Freud, asserts that psychoanalysis is interminable, because something about the human is incurable.

3. Freud too suggests that childhood memories cannot be interpreted independent of context. In his discussion of childhood memories in *The Psychopathology of Everyday Life*, Freud sees the significance of childhood memories as a concealing memory—that is, as an associative relation of their contents to a repressed thought—in which, "in order to attach the value of the concealing memory to an infantile reminiscence, it would be often necessary to present the entire life-history of the person concerned" (Freud 1914, 65).

4. See Stefania Pandolfo's discussion of Islam and the ethics of psychoanalysis in which she describes the ethical in Lacan as "the pursuit of lucidity and of a movement across the limit that he pondered through the figure of tragedy. . . . Remaining

mindful of the pole of desire is also, necessarily, a matter of encountering a limit, risking to venture beyond the economy of self-preservation, where an angle of visibility can be attained from the living contemplation of one's own disappearance" (Pandolfo 2018, 132).

5. See Piergiorgio Donatelli's discussion of emptiness and the ordinary (Donatelli 2006).

6. As is seen from the contest over facts within historiography of war in Korea, it is clear that it is not simply a question of gathering more facts as if they were stable and uncontested in the world.

7. Contrast this tension with Renato Rosaldo's *antropoesía* in *The Day of Shelly's Death: The Poetry and Ethnography of Grief* (2013), which we might say is an abandonment of professional anthropological theorizing in the attempt to give expression to and bear grief.

8. Compare this with Richard Moran's discussion of the third-person perspective on autobiography (Moran 2015).

9. Moving beyond dominant frameworks on the Korean War that have tended to focus on military history, geopolitics, and social movements in a world bifurcated by the consolidated identities of the South and the North, scholars have explored the everyday practices of survival during war and the routes by which everyday life is reclaimed in the wake of mass death and displacement. In oral history, for example, scholars have engaged in a "bottom-up reconstruction" of memory that takes the unit of the village as the starting point to describe how war left marks on status and hierarchy internal to village life (Yoon 1992; Yoon 2006). This scholarship has revealed the genres and vocabularies of everyday life that women draw upon to describe the pressures of war, such as extreme poverty and the precarity of one's kinship position (G. Kim 2012). Yet, oral history's privileging of the interview method tends to reconsolidate a discourse of trauma, such that the narration of "past" events can be seen as redemptive and therapeutic (G. Kim 2013; Yoon 2011). At the same time, because oral history tends to assume a concept of scale as a series of nested units (family, village, nation), the family is treated as a relatively independent sphere from the state.

10. In her brilliant ethnography with North Korean women migrants in South Korea, Sojung Kim shows how women engage in an "as-if" Chuseok ritual that is colored with disappointment, precisely because the frictions and explosive visceral tensions in kinship that normally permeate the ritual are not available to women whose kinship relations are physically cut off from them by partition (S. Kim 2019).

Interlude 1: Affliction and War in the Domestic

1. This sense of *fiction* is distinct from the assumptions about children's testimonies that shadow their speech in courts (Baxi 2013; Powell, Hlavka, and Mulla 2017). Children's testimonies are repeatedly called into question and substituted by fictions of law that hinge upon dominant myths of marginalized groups. In the literature on trauma and memory, however, trauma "renders events ineradicable," haunting the adult who fears that ordinary language is "inadequate" to express the pain they have witnessed (Kirmayer 1996). Thus, literature, as in the case of Charlotte Delbo, is seen as an attempt to make communicable that "deep memory" that cannot circulate in the public sphere, except through a leap of imagination (see Langer 1991).

Interlude 2: Homeward Bound

1. As Monica Kim shows in her remarkable historical monograph on the apparatus of interrogation during the Korean War, the politics of racialization permeated the United States military's techniques toward interrogation of Korean prisoners of war. Yet, even as the US military attempted to secure a narrative of racial superiority, they were awash in anxiety by what they were unable to absorb—the politics in and by Koreans and their claims to self-governance. Kim eschews a narrative of US empire and global cultural assimilation to instead show how the US military archive is permeated by its anxiety to secure that narrative (M. Kim 2019).

Part IV: Mother Tongue

1. For an astoundingly deep meditation on the nature of care that resonates with the twin impulses of life and lethality, see Arthur Kleinman's *The Soul of Care: The Moral Education of a Husband and a Doctor* (Kleinman 2019).

Epilogue: Seeing Like a Child

1. Contrast this writing from the feminine region with Adriana Cavarero's feminist philosophy of narration. Writing against the masculine impulse to author, Cavarero insists that women are "storytellers" whose narrations draw out the "who she is" rather than the "what it is"—women as subject rather than object. Yet, while Cavarero attempts to overcome the assumption of a unified self, she regrounds this unity as an insubstitutability "that persists in time because it continues to present itself in time" (Cavarero 2000, 64). Just a glimpse at the ethnographic record on biography and names, however, would surely have us rethink the notion of insubstitutability as a bedrock for the unified self (Day 2007).

2. Interestingly, this partially resonates with Stanley Cavell's description of the "search for the mother's gaze" in the film *Stella Dallas*. Cavell distinguishes the position of the woman from the immigrant: "But the position of women is neither that of exiles nor of immigrants: unlike the immigrant, the woman's problem is not one of not belonging but one of belonging, only on the wrong terms; unlike the exile, the woman is not between two different cultures but is at odds with the one in which she was born and is roughly in the process of transfiguring into one that does not exist, one as it were still in confinement" (Cavell 1996, 213). For Cavell, the immigrant child is one who is positioned between two different cultures in which entering into the host society and creating difference from the parents is the child's double bind of betrayal. Yet, as I reflect on my writings, it is not clear to me that immigrancy consisted of such a double bind.

Works Cited

Abraham, Nicolas. 1987. "Notes on the Phantom: A Complement to Freud's Metapsychology." *Critical Inquiry* 13 (Winter): 287–92.

Abraham, Nicolas, and Maria Torok. 1994. *The Shell and the Kernel: Renewals of Psychoanalysis*. Vol. 1. Chicago: University of Chicago Press.

Alber, Erdmute, Cati Coe, and Tatjana Thelen. 2013. *The Anthropology of Sibling Relations: Shared Parentage, Experience, and Exchange*. New York: Palgrave-Macmillan.

Assmann, Aleida. 2009. "Memory, Individual and Collective." In *The Oxford Handbook of Contextual Political Analysis*, edited by R. E. Goodin and C. Tilly, 210–26. Oxford: Oxford University Press.

Assmann, Jan. 1995. "Collective Memory and Cultural Identity." *New German Critique* 65 (Spring–Summer): 125–33.

———. 2007. *Cultural Memory and Early Civilization: Writing, Remembrance, and Political Imagination*. Cambridge: Cambridge University Press.

Bagaria, Swayam. 2017. "Interiorities of Memory." In *Book Forum—Nayanika Mookherjee's "The Spectral Wound: Sexual*

Violence, Public Memories, and the Bangladesh War of 1971," edited by Andrew Brandel. http://somatosphere.net/forumpost /interiorities-of-memory/.

Baik, Crystal Mun-Hye. 2020. *Reencounters: On the Korean War and Diasporic Memory Critique.* Philadelphia: Temple University Press.

Baxi, Pratiksha. 2013. *Public Secrets of Law: Rape Trials in India.* Oxford: Oxford University Press.

Behar, Ruth. 2014. *The Vulnerable Observer: Anthropology That Breaks Your Heart.* Boston: Beacon Press.

Benveniste, Emile. 1966. "De la subjectivité dans le langage." In *Problèmes de linguistique générale,* edited by E. Benveniste, 258–66. Paris: Gallimard.

Bluebond-Langner, Myra. 1978. *The Private Worlds of Dying Children.* Princeton, N.J.: Princeton University Press.

Bourgois, Philippe. 2005. "Missing the Holocaust." *Anthropological Quarterly* 78 (1): 89–123.

Carsten, Janet. 1997. *The Heat of the Hearth: The Process of Kinship in a Malay Fishing Community.* Oxford: Oxford University Press.

———. 2013. "What Kinship Does—and How." *HAU: Journal of Ethnographic Theory* 3 (2): 245–51.

———. 2018. "House-lives as Ethnography/Biography." *Social Anthropology* 26 (1): 103–16.

Carsten, Janet, Sophie Day, and Charles Stafford. 2018. "Introduction: Reason and Passion: The Parallel Worlds of Ethnography and Biography." *Social Anthropology* 26: 5–14.

Caruth, Cathy. 1996. *Unclaimed Experience: Trauma, Narrative, and History.* Baltimore: Johns Hopkins University Press.

———. 2015. *Listening to Trauma: Conversations in the Theory & Treatment of Catastrophic Experience.* Baltimore: Johns Hopkins University Press.

Cavell, Stanley. 1996. *Contesting Tears: The Hollywood Melodrama of the Unknown Woman.* Chicago: University of Chicago Press.

———. 2005. *Philosophy the Day after Tomorrow.* Cambridge, Mass.: Belknap Press of Harvard University Press.

———. 2008. "Time and Place for Philosophy." *Metaphilosophy* 39 (1): 51–61.

———. 2010. *Little Did I Know: Excerpts from Memory.* Stanford, Calif.: Stanford University Press.

Caverero, Adriana. 2000. *Relating Narratives: Storytelling and Selfhood.* New York: Routledge.

Cheng, Anne Anlin. 2001. *The Melancholy of Race.* Oxford: Oxford University Press.

Clifford, James, and George Marcus. 1986. *Writing Culture: The Poetics and Politics of Ethnography.* Berkeley: University of California Press.

Cumings, Bruce. 2011. *The Korean War: A History.* New York: Random House.

Das, Veena. 1998. "Wittgenstein and Anthropology." *Annual Review of Anthropology* 27: 171–95.

———. 2007. *Life and Words: Violence and the Descent into the Ordinary.* Berkeley: University of California Press.

———. 2015a. *Affliction: Health, Disease, Poverty.* New York: Fordham University Press.

———. 2015b. "What Does Ordinary Ethics Look Like?" In *Four Lectures on Ethics: Anthropological Perspectives,* edited by M. Lambek, V. Das, D. Fassin, and W. Keane, 53–126. HAU Books Masterclass Series. Chicago: HAU Books.

———. 2020. *Textures of the Ordinary: Doing Anthropology after Wittgenstein.* New York: Fordham University Press.

Day, Sophie. 2007. *On the Game: Women and Sex Work.* London: Pluto Press.

Derrida, Jacques. 1999. *Donner la mort.* Paris: Galilée.

Donatelli, Piergiorgio. 2006. "Bringing Truth Home: Mill, Wittgenstein, Cavell, and Moral Perfectionism." In *The Claim to Community: Stanley Cavell and Political Philosophy,* edited by A. Norris, 38–57. Stanford, Calif.: Stanford University Press.

Eng, David, and Shinhee Han. 2019. *Racial Melancholia, Racial Dissociation.* Durham, N.C.: Duke University Press.

Erll, Astri. 2011. "Locating Family in Cultural Memory Studies." *Journal of Comparative Family Studies* 42 (3): 303–18.

Freud, Sigmund. 1914. *Psychopathology of Everyday Life*. New York: Macmillan Company.

Freud, Sigmund. (1915) 1989. "Considérations actualles sur la guerre et la mort." In *Essais de psychanalyse*, edited by S. Freud. Paris: Payot.

Hadot, Pierre. 1995. *Philosophy as a Way of Life*. Malden, Mass.: Blackwell Publishing.

Han, Clara, and Andrew Brandel. 2019. "Genres of Witnessing: Narrative, Violence, Generations." *Ethnos*. https://doi.org/10.1080/00141844.2019.1630466.

Han, Kang. 2016. 흰 [The white book]. Translated by Deborah Smith. London: Portobello Books.

Hirsch, Marianne. 1997. *Family Frames: Photography, Narrative and Postmemory*. Cambridge, Mass.: Harvard University Press.

———. 2008. "The Generation of Postmemory." *Poetics Today* 29 (1): 103–28.

———. 2012. *The Generation of Postmemory: Writing and Visual Culture after the Holocaust*. New York: Columbia University Press.

Hong, Seunghei Clara. 2009. "Re-collecting Fragments: Towards a Politics of Memory in Partition Literature." PhD diss., University of Michigan.

Hwang, Su-kyoung. 2016. *Korea's Grievous War*. Philadelphia: University of Pennsylvania Press.

Jackson, Michael. 2006. *The Accidental Anthropologist: A Memoir*. Auckland, New Zealand: Longacre Press.

Kidron, Carol A. 2009. "Toward an Ethnography of Silence: The Lived Presence of the Past in the Everyday Life of Holocaust Trauma Survivors and Their Descendants in Israel." *Current Anthropology* 50 (1): 5–27.

Kim, Eun-shil. 2017. "The Politics of the Jeju 4.3 Holeomeong Bodies: 'Speaking' and Emotion as Embodied Language." *Korean Anthropology Review* 2: 1–42.

Kim, Gwi Ok. 2012. "Absence of Men and Presence of Women in Sijipsali during the Korean War." *Critical Review of History* 11: 402–33.

———. 2013. "Oral History and Healing—For the Possibility of
    Healing Trauma." *Journal of the Humanities for Unification*
    55: 131–65.
Kim, Monica. 2019. *The Interrogation Rooms of the Korean War:
    The Untold History*. Princeton, N.J.: Princeton University Press.
Kim, Nan. 2017. *Memory, Reconciliation, and Reunions in South
    Korea: Crossing the Divide*. Lanham, Md.: Lexington Books.
Kim, Seong Nae. 2013. "The Work of Memory: Ritual Laments
    of the Dead and Korea's Cheju Massacre." In *A Companion
    to the Anthropology of Religion*, edited by J. Boddy and
    M. Lambek, 223–38. New York: John Wiley & Sons.
Kim, Seong Nae. 2019. "Placing the Dead in the Postmemory of
    the Cheju Massacre in Korea." *Journal of Religion* 99 (1):
    80–97.
Kim, Sojung. 2019. "When Words Evaporate: Everyday Life of
    North Korean Migrant Women in South Korea." Methods
    Workshop, December 6, 2019. Department of Anthropology,
    Johns Hopkins University.
Kirmayer, Lawrence. 1996. "Landscapes of Memory." In *Tense
    Past: Cultural Essays in Trauma and Memory*, edited by
    P. Antze and M. Lambek, 173–98. New York: Routledge.
Kleinman, Arthur. 2019. *The Soul of Care: The Moral Education
    of a Husband and a Doctor*. New York: Viking.
Koh, Sungman. 2018. "Trans-Border Rituals for the Dead:
    Experiential Knowledge of Paternal Relatives after the Jeju
    4.3 Incident." *Journal of Korean Religions* 9 (1): 71–103.
Kwon, Heonik. 2010. *The Other Cold War*. New York: Columbia
    University Press.
———. 2015. "Korean War Mass Graves." In *Necropolitics: Mass
    Graves and Exhumations in the Age of Human Rights*, edited by
    F. Ferrándiz and A. C. G. M. Robben, 76–91. Philadelphia:
    University of Pennsylvania Press.
———. 2020. *After the Korean War: An Intimate History*.
    Cambridge: Cambridge University Press.
Lacan, Jacques. 1992. *The Ethics of Psychoanalysis, 1959–1960:
    The Seminar of Jacques Lacan*. London: Routledge.
———. 2002. *Écrits*. New York: W.W. Norton & Company.

Lane, Christopher. 1997. "The Testament of the Other: Abraham and Torok's Failed Expiation of Ghosts." *Diacritics* 27 (4): 3–29.

Langer, Lawrence. 1991. *Holocaust Testimonies: The Ruins of Memory*. New Haven, Conn.: Yale University Press.

Laugier, Sandra. 2011. "Matter and Mind: Cavell's (Concept of) Importance." *MLN* 126: 994–1003.

Lévi-Strauss, Claude. 1971. *L'homme nu*. Paris: Pion.

Marrati, Paola. 2011. "Childhood and Philosophy." *MLN* 126: 954–61.

Mitchell, Juliet. 2003. *Siblings*. Cambridge: Polity Press.

———. 2014. "Siblings and the Psychosocial." *Organisational & Social Dynamics* 14 (1): 1–12.

Mookherjee, Nayanika. 2015. *The Spectral Wound: Sexual Violence, Public Memories, and the Bangladesh War of 1971*. Durham, N.C.: Duke University Press.

Moran, Richard. 2015. *The Story of My Life: Narrative and Self-Understanding*. Milwaukee: Marquette University Press.

Nguyen, Viet Thanh. 2016. *Nothing Ever Dies: Vietnam and the Memory of War*. Cambridge, Mass.: Harvard University Press.

———. 2017. "Becoming Bilingual, or Notes on Numbness and Feeling." In *Flashpoints for Asian American Studies*, edited by C. J. Schlund-Vials, 299–307. New York: Fordham University Press.

Oh, Junghee. (1981) 2017. 유년의 뜰 [Garden of Childhood]. Seoul: Moonji Publishing Company.

Okazaki, Sumie, and Nancy Abelmann. 2018. *Korean American Families in Immigrant America: How Teens and Parents Navigate Race*. New York: New York University Press.

Pandolfo, Stefania. 2018. *Knot of the Soul: Madness, Psychoanalysis, Islam*. Chicago: University of Chicago Press.

Panourgiá, Neni. 1995. *Fragments of Death, Fables of Identity*. Madison: University of Wisconsin Press.

Powell, Amber Joy, Heather R. Hlavka, and Sameena Mulla. 2017. "Intersectionality and Credibility in Child Sexual Assault Trials." *Gender & Society* 31 (4): 457–80.

Rechtman, Richard. 1996. "Anthropologie et psychoanalyse: un débat hors sujet?" *Journal des Anthropologues* 64–65 (1): 65–86.

———. 2017. "From an Ethnography of the Everyday to Writing Echoes of Suffering." *Medicine Anthropology Theory* 4 (3): 130–42.

Reynolds, Pamela. 2012. *War in Worcester: Youth and the Apartheid State*. New York: Fordham University Press.

Rosaldo, Renato. 2013. *The Day of Shelly's Death: The Poetry and Ethnography of Grief*. Durham, N.C.: Duke University Press.

Saito, Naoko. 2009. "Ourselves in Translation: Stanley Cavell and Philosophy as Autobiography." *Journal of Philosophy of Education* 43 (2): 253–67.

Schwab, Gabriele. 2010. *Haunting Legacies: Violent Histories and Transgenerational Trauma*. New York: Columbia University Press.

Strathern, Marilyn. 1987. "The Limits of Auto-anthropology." In *Anthropology at Home*, edited by A. Jackson, 16–37. London: Tavistock Publications.

Trawick, Margaret. 2007. *Enemy Lines: Warfare, Childhood, and Play in Batticaloa*. Berkeley: University of California Press.

Waterston, Alisse, and Barbara Rylko-Bauer. 2006. "Out of the Shadows of History and Memory: Personal Family Narratives in Ethnographies of Rediscovery." *American Ethnologist* 33 (3): 397–412.

Yassa, Maria. 2002. "Nicolas Abraham and Maria Torok—the Inner Crypt." *Scandinavian Psychoanalytic Review* 25: 82–91.

Yoon, Taek-Lim. 1992. "The Politics of Memory in the Ethnographic History of a 'Red' Village in South Korea." *Korea Journal* 32 (4): 65–79.

———. 2006. "Ordinary People's War Stories." *Review of Korean Studies* 92 (2): 33–56.

———. 2011. "Oral History Interview and Historical Trauma: Possibility for Combining the Task of Seeking Truths with Healing Historical Wounds." *Studies in Humanities* 30 (9): 381–406.

CLARA HAN is Associate Professor of Anthropology at Johns Hopkins University. She is the author of *Life in Debt: Times of Care and Violence in Neoliberal Chile* (2012) and a co-editor of *Living and Dying in the Contemporary World: A Compendium* (2015).

Thinking from Elsewhere

CPSIA information can be obtained
at www.ICGtesting.com
Printed in the USA
JSHW031143151122
33234JS00002B/149

ANTHROPOLOGY | ASIAN AMERICAN STUDIES

"*Seeing Like a Child* is an extraordinary book, bursting with critical insight and affective power. Han vividly explores how war and migration are dispersed into a domestic life marked by small corrosions, devastating loss, and tiny solidarities. Courageously probing the plasticity of self and lifeworld, the anthropologist illuminates the fragile but deeply meaningful yearnings of her family's memorable characters. A must-read."

—João Biehl, author of *Vita: Life in a Zone of Social Abandonment*

"With this deeply moving intimate history, Clara Han reclaims an important legacy of modern anthropology: its capacity to connect the personal with the world-historical. *Seeing Like a Child* is an audacious attempt to restore kinship as a vital category in historical and political inquiry and a must-read for anyone interested in discovering how much of the world is involved in bringing up a child."

—Heonik Kwon, author of *After the Korean War: An Intimate History*

In this deeply moving narrative, Clara Han explores how the catastrophic event of the Korean War is dispersed into domestic life. Han writes from inside her childhood memories as the daughter of parents whose migrations—from the North to the South of Korea and then to the United States—frayed familial ties. At the same time, she writes as an anthropologist whose fieldwork has taken her to the devastated worlds of her parents—to Korea and to the Korean language—allowing her to find and found kinship relationships broken in war and illness. A fascinating counterpoint to the project of testimony that seeks to transmit a narrative to future generations *Seeing Like a Child* sees the inheritance of familial memories of violen as embedded in how the child inhabits her everyday life.

Clara Han is Associate Professor of Anthropology at Johns Hopkins University.

THINKING FROM ELSEWHERE
Clara Han and Bhrigupati Singh, series editors

FORDHAM UNIVERSITY PRESS
New York   www.fordhampress.com

Cover image: Park Daa Won, *Now Here - Becoming* (2015). Used by permission of the artist. Cover design by Maarten Ottens

ISBN 978-0-8232-8946
9 780823 289462

W9-AST-64!